In a Day's Work

In a Day's Work

The Fight to End Sexual Violence Against
America's Most Vulnerable Workers

Bernice Yeung

THE NEW PRESS

NEW YORK
LONDON

Letter on pages 197–199 used by permission of Georgina Hernández.

Requests for permission to reproduce selections from this book
should be mailed to: Permissions Department, The New Press,
120 Wall Street, 31st floor, New York, NY 10005.

Published in the United States by The New Press, New York, 2018
Distributed by Two Rivers Distribution

ISBN 978-1-62097-316-5 (e-book)

LIBRARY OF CONGRESS CATALOGING-IN-PUBLICATION DATA

Names: Yeung, Bernice, author.
Title: In a day's work : the fight to end sexual violence
against America's most vulnerable workers / Bernice Yeung.
Description: New York : New Press, [2018]
Identifiers: LCCN 2017053297 | ISBN 9781620973158 (hc : alk. paper)
Subjects: LCSH: Sexual harassment—United States. | Women
foreign workers—Crimes against—United States. | Women
immigrants—Crimes against—United States. | Sexual abuse
victims—United States. | Sex crimes—United States. |
Violence in the workplace—United States.
Classification: LCC HD6060.5.U5 Y48 2018 | DDC 362.88086/910973—
dc23 LC record available at https://lccn.loc.gov/2017053297

The New Press publishes books that promote and enrich public discussion and
understanding of the issues vital to our democracy and to a more equitable world.
These books are made possible by the enthusiasm of our readers; the support
of a committed group of donors, large and small; the collaboration of our many
partners in the independent media and the not-for-profit sector; booksellers, who
often hand-sell New Press books; librarians; and above all by our authors.

www.thenewpress.com

Book design and composition by dix!
This book was set in Fairfield LH

Printed in the United States of America

2   4   6   8   10   9   7   5   3   1

3601805718 8120

To the women who shared their stories
with us, and to those who couldn't.

And for my father, who has shown me the
importance of crossing borders.

These places of possibility within ourselves are dark because they are ancient and hidden; they have survived and grown strong through darkness. Within these deep places, each one of us holds an incredible reserve of creativity and power, of unexamined and unrecorded emotion and feeling. The woman's place of power within each of us is neither white nor surface; it is dark, it is ancient, and it is deep.

—Audre Lorde, from "Poetry Is Not a Luxury"

Contents

In a Day's Work

Introduction

The Weight of Silence

It neared dusk as we drove into the depths of a small community built around farms and fields of the Pacific Northwest. The clouds were low and gray as we navigated a busy two-lane road that led in and out of town, past a Mexican restaurant, a diner, and a farm-supply store.

Just beyond a pizza parlor, we turned off the main road and continued past the length of a parking lot until we found a cluster of one-story brick apartments. In one of them lived a farmworker who we will call Rosa. She was the reason my colleague Grace and I had come to town.

As journalists, Grace and I were on a reporting team working to expose a long-held but open secret: immigrant women in some of the most financially precarious jobs—many of whom are undocumented—were being targeted for sexual abuse by their superiors. We wanted to meet with Rosa because, according to a lawsuit that she and her family had filed, she had been sexually harassed at work. Worse, Rosa's sister had been repeatedly raped by a supervisor there.

Reading the case file had left me internalizing the weight of their story. The detailed descriptions of the rapes were difficult to get through. She said her supervisor had violated her in a farm shed while he held gardening shears to her throat. He pulled her hair or slapped her while he raped her because he said she wasn't putting enough effort into it. Then he coerced her into silence by threatening to kill her children in Mexico or by reminding her of the power he had to fire her sister and brother, who also worked at the same farm. The supervisor knew that for workers not authorized to be in the country, the prospect of losing a job was almost as menacing as a death threat.

This case exemplified the phenomenon our reporting team was seeking to uncover: how immigration status and poverty are leveraged against female workers to hold them hostage in jobs where they are being sexually abused. Rosa's sister seemed too traumatized for us to approach directly, so Grace and I had decided to talk to Rosa first.

We parked the car and made our way into a grassy courtyard in search of the right apartment. We circled the complex and stopped at a door facing the street to check the number against our notes. This was it. We knocked.

The woman who answered had a broad face and high cheekbones. She still wore the jeans and fleece vest that she had put on before starting a shift at an egg production plant nearby. Grace and I introduced ourselves and told Rosa why we were there. She surveyed us warily. When we mentioned the name of the person who'd suggested we contact her, she reluctantly beckoned us inside.

We followed Rosa through the living room, which had been partitioned by curtains to create a third makeshift bedroom, and into the kitchen. Rosa was in the middle of making dinner, resuscitating leftover *mole* sauce that a friend had given her. As the pot bubbled on the stove, we sat down at the table to get to know one another. Our conversation spanned the mundane to the meaningful: cooking techniques, her children, and her journey from Mexico through the desert to the United States. After a time, she insisted that we share in the meal. She had added chicken to the sauce, which was rich and hearty.

Before the end of the evening, Rosa agreed to speak with us about what had happened to both her and her sister at the farm where they had worked. Like many of the women we encountered, she said she wanted to bring attention to an untenable problem and hoped that by doing so, she would help other women.

But as we talked, a thought occurred to her. Before she agreed to a recorded interview for possible radio and television broadcast, she had some questions. How would taking such a public stance affect her job? More important, what if the supervisor who had raped her sister found out and decided to retaliate against them? She added that she had run into him just the week before at a *quinceañera* and he'd given her a dirty look. Before that, she had spotted him at the local Walmart.

Grace and I didn't have any answers for Rosa, and we told her so. In fact, as reporters, we could promise her little except the possibility of protecting her identity and telling her story with fidelity. We suggested that she talk to someone who she trusted about whether she should agree to continue speaking with us or not. About a week later, we got word that despite her altruistic impulses, Rosa had decided not to proceed.

It was easy for us to understand why. On our third and last visit with Rosa, she had taken us into her bedroom, packed with cleaning supplies and beauty products. There, standing next to her bed, she pulled out her phone to show us pictures of her two teenage kids. She had left them with her mother eight years ago when she had come to America in search of work to support them. In the way that her smile widened at their image, it was clear: her kids and her ability to provide for them were the sun around which she revolved.

When Rosa and everyone else in her situation are asked to make it publicly known that they've been raped or otherwise sexually assaulted, the stakes for them are impossibly high. The potential collective good is weighed against what is immediately and urgently necessary. Because there is no assurance that speaking out will be met with protection from future or collateral harm, the only rational thing to do is to say nothing. After meeting Rosa, I came to understand why so many sexually abused workers have for so long abided in silence.

Grace and I had gone looking for Rosa in the fall of 2012, but the effort to uncover the stories of women farmworkers who had been sexually abused on the job had begun several years before. It had started with Linsay Rousseau Burnett, a journalism graduate student at the University of California at Berkeley who had taken an internship at a national television network in the summer of 2009. She had been tasked with reporting on child farm labor, and it was on a trip to rural North Carolina that she discovered another story that urgently needed telling.

During a visit to a migrant farmworker community clinic, Rousseau Burnett met the outreach coordinator, who told the journalism student her own story. She had been smuggled from Mexico and brought to the United States to work in the fields. Her coyote was also the supervisor at the farm, and he had exploited his authority by raping her repeatedly. She had gotten pregnant by him eight times, and for years he had used threats and intimidation to keep her quiet. She told Rousseau Burnett she was not the only one.

It was a story almost too extreme to contemplate. When the television network declined to pursue it, one of Rousseau Burnett's journalism school advisors, the veteran investigative reporter Lowell Bergman, encouraged her to continue working on the story once she returned to the university. Back in California, Rousseau Burnett dug into the topic and found that it was a systemic issue. "It came about by hearing one person's story in North Carolina," Rousseau Burnett says. "And we kept asking the question and we kept hearing from other people that this was a problem."

As I would soon find out, this was a hard story to tackle. After years of reporting, Rousseau Burnett graduated to pursue jobs in journalism and eventually acting. Before she left the university, she gave her status updates and drafts to Bergman, who runs the Investigative Reporting Program at UC Berkeley. Another journalism student named Rosa Ramírez picked up the reporting for a time, but she, too, graduated before the project could be completed.

It was a story that Bergman continued to believe was worth telling, and it was a topic that he knew few media organizations would take on. He decided to assemble a team and find the funding to see the project through.

In 2012, as a journalist with The Center for Investigative Reporting, I was given the opportunity to join that reporting team, which was made up of journalists at UC Berkeley's Investigative Reporting Program and at KQED-FM, the Northern California public radio station. The project, which we called "Rape in the Fields," resulted in TV documentaries in English and Spanish for PBS Frontline and Univision, as well as bilingual public-radio pieces and newspaper articles.[1]

In more than a year of reporting, we found that, from the meatpacking plants of Iowa to the lettuce fields of California to the apple orchards of Washington, women expected to encounter sexual harassment, assault, and even rape at work.

As outsiders, we were shocked, but this was a problem that had been known within the farmworker community for generations. The confluence of economic precariousness, language barriers, shame, fear, and immigration status had created a workplace where women sexually abused believed they had no choice but to try to deflect or somehow endure the violence.

We studied the sexual harassment cases that the federal government had brought against agricultural employers since the late 1990s—a little more than forty lawsuits at the time—and we found that most cases involved multiple workers who had been sexually assaulted or raped by the same supervisors. Most involved claims of retaliation once the workers had worked up the nerve to complain. None of the civil cases had resulted in a criminal prosecution.

Even as we were in the process of seeking out the stories of farmworkers, we learned that this dynamic was not confined to America's fields, orchards, and packing plants. In one of our first interviews on the farmworker project, we were told by William R. Tamayo, a government attorney, that the same problem existed in the janitorial industry.

That tip led to a follow-up piece, "Rape on the Night Shift," in which the reporting team took a close look at an industry that operates in a largely underground or subcontracted fashion, where companies operate in obscurity and workers clean in anonymous buildings that government regulators and journalists rarely visit.[2]

Following eighteen months of reporting, we found that regardless of whether cleaners were hired by large companies or tiny, off-the-radar firms, the dynamics are similar to farm work. It is a job done by immigrants laboring in isolation for tiny paychecks, and if a supervisor decides to abuse their position, the combination of immigration status, financial constraints, and shame conspires to keep victims silent. We also found that some companies were dismissive of reports of sexual violence. In one case, the cleaning company told the offending supervisor to investigate himself. In another, the company ignored the eyewitness report of a church volunteer who said he'd seen a supervisor physically assault a female worker.

This book draws from that body of reporting from 2012 to 2015. I have also expanded on it by updating various case studies, and exploring how the same unfortunate pattern plays out among domestic workers, those who cook, clean, and care for families behind the locked doors of private homes. Their vulnerability to sexual violence echoed what we had heard from farmworkers and janitors. In their isolated workplaces, it was frequently their direct employers who groped them or propositioned them for sex. Domestic workers also face a unique legal hurdle: Because they have been purposely excluded from various federal labor laws, there is not always a clear path to recourse for workplace abuses such as sexual harassment and assault.

After looking at various industries that hire the most vulnerable workers, I've been forced to conclude that low-wage immigrants laboring in isolation are at unique risk of sexual assault and harassment. While it is not possible to know how often these abuses happen, they are not anomalies. The federal government estimates that about fifty workers are sexually assaulted each day, and in the industries that hire newcomers to the country in exchange for meager paychecks, such assault is a known and familiar workplace hazard.

As this book documents, however, there are few meaningful efforts to prevent workplace sexual violence before it starts. Instead, we unrealistically expect women with the most to lose to seek recourse by reporting the problem after the fact. The legal system—through filing a civil lawsuit or a criminal case—is often viewed as the clearest way to demand accountability. Workers can also go to their employers and unions to demand redress. Making a formal complaint helps emphasize that there can be consequences for this type of abusive conduct. But they are only part of the solution. These approaches are inherently reactive, and they require the confrontation of systemic roadblocks—such as deeply flawed notions of credibility—that create challenges to satisfying or just outcomes. They also do not, as esteemed law professor Kimberlé Williams Crenshaw has argued, consider the "intersectionality" of these workers' experiences as women of color or immigrants, and how these identities impact the way they are perceived, how they might react, and the type of help they might need when faced with gender-based violence.[3]

Meanwhile, we know that prevention is possible. Decades of

empirical research offers clear direction. While there are some heartening efforts to incorporate this research into worker training and advocacy programs, employers and policy makers have largely chosen not to use it.

In addition, advocates for female workers have for decades tried to make the case that sexual assault at work should not be dismissed and marginalized by employers and the government simply because it has historically been perceived as a "women's issue." Instead, they argue, gender-based violence should be viewed in the same way as other forms of on-the-job physical violence so that prevention plans are implemented, the government takes a proactive role in enforcement, and workers have an avenue for demanding accountability. Recently there have been successful efforts at the state level to recast this problem as an issue that can be averted through public policy. Employers may worry that these efforts are overly cumbersome, but this is the paradigm from which prevention can begin.

In the end, this book seeks to excavate and disrupt an unacceptable set of circumstances that promote silence. Whether victims of sexual violence choose to share their stories publicly or not is a deeply personal question, and there should never be a mandate that they do. By recounting the experiences of the immigrant women who have taken the improbable step of reporting workplace sexual harassment and assault, I am asking why we give so little real help to those who courageously come forward?

It took seven months of reporting for "Rape in the Fields" before we met Maricruz Ladino. She had worked at a lettuce farm in Salinas, California, where her supervisor propositioned her and gave her unwanted massages. When she rebuffed him, he threatened her. "He told me to keep in mind that he had the power to decide how much longer I could work there," she recalls. "I was a single mother and I was scared. I was worried that if I didn't do what he wanted me to do, I would lose my job, the source of income for my daughters and my mother, who was already alone."

Then one day in 2006, Ladino's supervisor told her he wanted her to come with him to check the crops in a remote field. That's where he raped her. For years, she never told anyone about what had happened, but she began to find solace in writing letters to her deceased father in her journal. Through these epistolary conversations, Ladino realized that her father had taught her not to stand for the kind of injustice that had happened to her—either for herself or for others.

"There came a time when I told myself, 'No more,'" she says. "I am seeing that this type of thing did not only happen to me. It was happening to many, many more women and if I stay quiet then it is going to continue happening. That is why I now prefer to talk about it. I hope that many people see themselves in me and they won't stay quiet anymore."

Workplace sexual violence is not limited to immigrant women in low-wage jobs, but workers like Ladino have particular reasons for burying their experiences.[4] Ladino thinks that the combination of undocumented immigration status and worries about losing a job serve as a powerful muzzle. "The biggest factor is fear," she says. "Fear that the threats of deportation and the threats of losing our jobs will be real."

These fears have only expanded. The political and social climate has changed markedly since we first spoke to Ladino in 2013. President Donald Trump's immigration-related agenda seeks to tighten our borders, limit immigration, and expel noncitizens. Immigration authorities are arresting people without papers at a faster clip at their homes, jobs, and courthouses. There is a greater tolerance for rhetoric that promotes white supremacy and sexism and a simultaneous rollback of labor policies that make it harder for workers to exercise rights meant to protect them from exploitation.

In this context, the experiences of the immigrant women featured in this book become even harder to unearth. At the same time, it is more important than ever that they are heard. By speaking up when innumerable external forces demanded silence and secrecy, these women workers are a model of resilience and resistance worthy of emulation.

If silence dominated before, we cannot allow it to prevail now.

1

Finding the Most Invisible Cases

The Southern California sky dims as Vicky Márquez, one of America's unlikeliest undercover workplace investigators, zooms southward along Interstate 5 in her Honda SUV. Syrupy Spanish love songs blast from her stereo as the GPS on her phone directs her toward a monotonous landscape of Orange County office parks.

It's a late winter day in 2015 and Márquez is racing against rush hour, slowed by red brake lights before the traffic inexplicably speeds up again. She looks to gain seconds by dodging between lanes, swerving with inches to spare. "I'm kind of a crazy driver," she admits.

She is also on something of a mission. Márquez works for the Maintenance Cooperation Trust Fund (MCTF), a little-known nonprofit with an unwieldy name and the pressing goal of fighting labor exploitation among janitors working the graveyard shift. That evening, Márquez is on the road to the first of a half-dozen office parks that she will visit that night to make sure that cleaners are being treated fairly by their bosses. With her glasses, curled-under bangs, and pastel sweaters, Márquez looks more like a retired librarian than a labor rights crusader. On tiptoe, she stands less than five feet tall.

Márquez conducts surprise inspections in the heart of Southern

California sprawl at least once a week. About a dozen of her co-workers are out doing the same throughout the state, but it is a job that few government agencies bother to do.

It is work that Márquez believes in, a cause she has lived. For sixteen years, she worked as a janitor herself. She has a story that in many ways echoes what she hears from the women she meets during her undercover operations. She faced an economic dead end in her home country of El Salvador, which had endured more than a decade of war. She and her husband decided that one of them had to find work elsewhere to support their three children, and since Márquez wasn't able to find a job at home, she was the one who made her way to California, where she had a niece.

When Márquez arrived in Los Angeles, she didn't speak much English—she still doesn't—and for the first few months, she worked as a babysitter and then at a hair salon. She needed a steadier paycheck, so when someone told her about a job with a cleaning company, she took it. The work was rough, and she had to work more hours than she was paid for, but she managed to send some of the money back home. For a time, it was a necessary if imperfect solution. More than two decades have passed. Her children have grown up. She has made a separate life in Los Angeles, and now, toward the end of her working years, she has found a job that suits her.

After forty minutes of frenetic driving, Márquez takes an exit toward the city center of San Clemente. Her target, a series of office parks, looms in the distance. During the day, these buildings are blinding in their blandness, but in the dark, they are almost beautiful in the way that they glow from within. Márquez circles the parking lot slowly, observing. She pulls into a parking space near the building deepest into the office park and thrusts a stack of papers into a bulging black bag that she swings onto her shoulder as she climbs out of the car.

She tests the front door of the office building. She has arrived early enough in the evening that it swings open with ease, leading to a nondescript lobby and a bank of elevators. It's not always so easy to gain entrance. If the doors are locked, Márquez has her strategies, which the organization she works for has developed over more than fifteen years of undercover work. She might, for example, station herself near the service exits or the dumpsters, where she knows the night-shift cleaners will eventually present themselves. In supermarkets or guarded high rises, she will sweetly ask for the janitor. If the person she's talking to wants to judge her by appearances and assume that she's looking for a job, so be it.

Tonight she walks into the building without delay, her heels click-clacking across the shiny tile lobby. Márquez's first move is to look for bathrooms or supply closets, two places she knows she is likely to find a janitor. She moves past the elevators to a rear hallway, where she finds María García, a cleaner holding a mop next to a bucket of murky, citrus-smelling water.

Márquez greets the cleaner brightly in Spanish. García is on the clock and she responds brusquely, almost warily. Márquez knows from experience that every minute spent chitchatting means a later shift and a longer night. The inspector doesn't waste time on small talk. Setting her massive black purse on the hallway drinking fountains, Márquez extracts a packet of papers that she passes to the cleaner. The investigator explains that she works for a nonprofit organization, the Maintenance Cooperation Trust Fund, which helps janitors make sure they get paid what they are owed and helps them solve problems with issues like immigration.

García sets the mop aside. Her mother needs some immigration help, she tells Márquez. The petite investigator nods, flipping to a page in the packet with information about recent changes to U.S. immigration policy, and tells her that the organization can provide her with more resources.

Now that she has García's attention, Márquez asks a few more questions that will help her get a feel for whether the janitor is being treated fairly at work: Does García get paid in cash or with a check on a regular basis? A check every two weeks, García says. Márquez nods, approvingly. Is she given regular breaks? Yes.

Does she have to pay for her own cleaning supplies? Well, García tells her, sometimes what the company gives her is not enough, so she has to buy a few more bottles of bleach. Márquez tells her that it's the company's responsibility to provide her with the supplies that she needs, and encourages García to ask for more bleach instead of buying it herself.

Then Márquez goes in to close the deal. *"Tu teléfono, mija?"* Márquez asks, sweetly but firmly. As García recites her phone number, Márquez scribbles it into a black notebook. *"Y tu dirección?"* Márquez takes down García's address next to the phone number.

Gathering workers' contact information is Márquez's ultimate goal during these brief encounters. The Maintenance Cooperation Trust Fund is one of only a handful of organizations in the country keeping careful tabs on the practices of non-unionized cleaning companies—some of which are largely untraceable, because they work entirely in the black market. Through these impromptu meetings, the organization has generated a database of workers who can give firsthand testimony about whether these hard-to-track companies are following labor laws.

García doesn't know it as she stands in the hallway with her bucket and mop, but Márquez will call or visit her at home in the early afternoon when most night janitors have not yet left for work. At these follow-up meetings, Márquez will remind García that she is there to help solve problems she is facing at work. If García doesn't pick up the phone or answer the door, Márquez will keep trying until she makes contact with her two and then eventually three times.

It's a process that can take months, but this is the long, slow dance that is necessary to build trust among workers who labor on the outermost fringes, in low-paying and invisible industries

like night-shift janitorial work. In this way, Márquez and her co-
workers have turned up problems among a group of workers unlikely to make formal complaints. They have found cases where
workers weren't being paid minimum wage or overtime, or where
they weren't given a single break during eight-hour shifts. Since
1999, they have helped collect more than $26 million for janitors
who were being abused at work.

In the past five years, Márquez has met hundreds of janitors
and tried to help dozens of them with their job problems. She has
discovered that a lot can happen in places where no one is looking.
Still, she didn't realize the extent of it until she met a young cleaner
named Georgina Hernández.

The day after a long night of visiting janitors throughout Orange
County, Vicky Márquez is in her car again. This time, she is
headed to a part of Los Angeles where corner stores sell tacos and
the neighborhood grocery store bakery offers a dizzying array of
pan dulce.

She stops at a white corner apartment building, passing through
the entrance to knock on the first door on the right. Hernández
answers, wearing her long, straight hair tied back from her round,
sweet face. Hernández's four-year-old daughter runs out to say
hello in plastic teal princess pumps.

Hernández met Márquez three years ago when the inspector
was making her weekly rounds through the city to visit janitors
on the job. Hernández was working at a movie theater sweeping
up popcorn between the seats. The two have stayed in constant
contact, even after Hernández moved on to clean the warehouse
where lunches are packaged for local public school students. Her
conditions are much better than when she first met Márquez. She
was earning a steady minimum-wage paycheck that adds up to a
little over $17,000 a year. Her hours were stable, and she was being
paid reliably for the hours that she worked.

On her salary, Hernández cannot afford her own apartment, so she splits one with four other newcomers from Mexico who all have their own minimum-wage-or-less jobs. Even in its less populated state that day, the apartment is a display of immigrant industry. Racks of thrift store clothes block the front windows. In her off hours, Hernández sets up shop at a local church to sell blouses, kids' clothes, and button-down shirts at a slight markup. Hernández has also tucked industrial-size pots away in the kitchen. A native of Puebla, the *mole* capital of Mexico, she has found that she can supplement her income by making big batches of the sauce for parties and weddings out of the little kitchen adjoining the living room. She parses her earnings as tightly as possible. In addition to the expense of living in California with her daughter, Hernández wires as much money as she can to Mexico to support the six children she left behind.

The afternoon that Hernández first met Vicky Márquez, the cleaner was coming to the end of her shift at the movie theater. Hernández had many concerns to report. For the first month and a half on the job, she had never received a paycheck. The amount of work that her supervisor expected—sweeping the sticky floors of the theater, cleaning the bathrooms, vacuuming the expanse of hallway carpeting—took longer than the eight hours listed on her paycheck. "We worked against time," Hernández says. And no matter how many hours she put in, the pay was always the same: $300 a week.

All of this work made Hernández sleepless and anemic, but she hadn't complained to anyone because it wasn't clear whom she should talk to, and she didn't have the time to figure it out. She also made the calculation that as someone without immigration papers, she was easy to replace.

When Márquez found Hernández at the theater, Hernández remembers being struck by the way the investigator spoke to her, so gently and sweetly, like an aunt. Márquez seemed to understand so much about her without much explanation. When Márquez asked

Hernández questions about whether she was getting paid regularly or whether she was getting extra money for working more than eight hours at a time, Hernández admitted aloud for the first time that she had not been. The cleaner added that the checks never seemed to add up to all of the work she was doing. Before Márquez left, she took down Hernández's phone number and told the janitor that she would check in with her again.

On her next visit with Hernández, Márquez looked at the cleaner's pay stubs and compared them to the work hours that Hernández had written down in a notebook. They didn't match up. When Márquez asked why Hernández hadn't written down any time for breaks, Hernández said that it was because she wasn't being given time to eat or rest during her shift.

Márquez explained that all of this was against the law, and for Hernández, it was an affirmation to know that what had felt so wrong was actually illegal. "From then on I started to talk to Vicky," Hernández says. "I would ask her, 'What could I do? How can I find help?' She would give me advice, little by little, about where I could ask for help and who I could talk to."

Márquez and the Maintenance Cooperation Trust Fund eventually helped Hernández and some of her co-workers file a complaint with California's labor commissioner. It would take nearly a year but the two cleaning companies that Hernández worked for at the theater—one went out of business and another took over the contract—were eventually fined nearly $1 million by the state of California for failing to pay minimum wage and overtime, and for not giving their workers rest or meal breaks.[1]

Hernández didn't stick with that cleaning company for too long. It had assigned her to clean a hotel restaurant, where she had spent hours scrubbing a hotel restaurant, the adjoining bar, and its two greasy kitchens. She was supposed to work from 10:00 p.m. until 6:00 a.m., but "sometimes that was a lie," Hernández says. "It wasn't enough time to finish all of the work."

The janitorial supervisor for the company that cleaned the hotel itself said he'd noticed that she was a good worker, and he told her that he could give her a higher-paying job cleaning the lobby and the exterior of the hotel. Hernández hated scrubbing the oily kitchens and lifting the heavy rubber floor mats, so with his help, she filled out an application. He hired her soon afterward.

That job came with bigger problems. From nearly her first day, she says, her supervisor flirted with her and tried to convince her to have sex with him. She rebuffed him, and he retaliated by giving her more work to do. When his advances didn't stop, she hid from him in the bathrooms. Undeterred, he'd follow her into the women's restroom or call her on her cell phone to find out where she was so he could talk to her.

His demands quickly became violent. Less than a week into the new job, Hernández says her boss told her that he needed to talk to her privately about her work in his car. This made Hernández uncomfortable, but he said, "You need this job, don't you?"

He instructed Hernández to meet him on the upper level of the hotel parking garage. She tried to ward him off but he ignored her. At about 1:00 a.m., he called her and said that he was waiting for her. Worried about losing her job, she went to see him. When she got to the parking lot, he told her to get into his car.

She hesitated but he was the boss. She did what she was told.

The supervisor drove them to a higher floor of the garage, where it was darker and it would be harder to find them. After he parked, Hernández's boss began to touch her legs, she says. She told him she didn't want to go on, and he replied that he'd give her more days off and better pay. Hernández told him that she didn't want more days off; she had taken the job because she wanted to work for her paycheck. When he began touching her breasts, she became afraid. Then, she says, he took off her pants.

As he forced himself on her, she panicked and her body froze. When he was done, the supervisor asked her to put in a request for an extra shift that week so that he could take her to a hotel and they could spend more than just a few minutes in a car. Hernández tried to protest and told him she couldn't do it. He assured her that there would be perks to it. He would pay her for the shift and make sure she received seven shifts that week. "You're delicious," he told her before driving her to a lower level of the parking garage. He told her to go into the building first. He followed a while later to avoid detection.

Hernández never requested an extra shift. She didn't immediately tell anyone what her supervisor had done. The shame of it was too much, and she knew it would be a challenge to quickly find a new job as an undocumented worker who couldn't read or write. And as someone who had been sexually abused as a teenager, she had learned how to push on after incidents like this.

About a week later, Hernández's supervisor told her to meet him again. When she said no and tried to quit, he threatened to hurt Hernández and her daughter, and added that if she wanted to stay in the country, she needed to keep him happy. This time he drove them to a motel.

Her supervisor continued to exploit the pretext of work to abuse Hernández. On one of her nights off, he called her incessantly until she picked up the phone. He said he needed her to work that night and because Hernández didn't have a car, he was on his way to pick her up. Hernández hurried to get herself ready for work, but once she was in his car, her supervisor didn't take the freeway to the hotel as she expected. Instead, he drove to the motel. She cried and tried to climb out of the car, but he pulled her out of the car and into a room by her hair, where she says he forced her to have sex with him again.

Afterwards, her supervisor once again warned her not to tell anyone what had happened. She would have stayed silent anyway. She thought her family and friends would never believe her or would think she had brought it upon herself.

Hernández says that at the time, she didn't think there was a way
out of her supervisor's trap. "There's no way to defend yourself," she
says. "There's no way to say no. When you need the job, you become the victim of others. That's why you deal with everything, all
of the harassment. You deal with discrimination, everything. You
deal with it because you need the job."

For the next few weeks, she reported to work at the hotel as
usual, making it a point to avoid her supervisor. He managed to find
her, however, either to remind her how much she needed the job or
to chastise her for being so cold during their encounters. Finally,
he came to her with an ultimatum: she had to decide whether she
wanted to keep her job or not. If she did, he would continue to have
certain expectations of her.

Hernández felt hopeless, unmoored. She was having migraines
and panic attacks. She dreaded his next demand. But she couldn't
agree to the abuse. When he confronted her again, she told him
that she had self-respect and she would not have sex with him to
keep her job.

Her supervisor began his revenge. He yelled at her in front of her
coworkers and disciplined her for supposedly leaving used tissues
in the lobby. Mortified, she cried. The campaign of yelling continued, and then she says her supervisor began to sabotage her work,
throwing trash in areas that she had already cleaned and then dis-
ciplining her for it.

The rapes had been horrific violations, but they had happened
in private. Now her supervisor was publicly impugning her work,
and her job was still at risk. She felt lost and compromised, but she
swallowed how she felt and continued to drag herself to work.

She tried not to show how damaged she felt, even though she felt
she was cracking inside. Feeling desperate, Hernández decided to
speak to the cleaning company about the assaults. She had seen
her supervisor try to hug and flirt with another cleaner, so together

the women called Human Resources to make a complaint. But Hernández says nothing changed.

Almost two months into the job, Hernández called in sick one evening. It was all her supervisor needed to remind her that he still had the upper hand. The next day, he fired her.

Hernández didn't leave the house for days. She had headaches and couldn't sleep. The nausea she felt only continued to intensify. The truth was hard to face: she was pregnant.

Hernández had hit the edge of what she could handle on her own. Depleted and sobbing, she sought out the only person she could trust. Vicky Márquez remembers how Hernández sounded that afternoon. She was crying and her voice was faded and anguished. Márquez had rushed to Hernández's apartment, but the cleaner said they could not talk there. "I'm afraid that the walls will hear, and I don't want anyone to hear me," she said to Márquez.

They talked for a while in Márquez's car. "Something has happened that I don't want to have to tell you, Vicky," Hernández began, "Something terrible." She was inconsolable and could not go on. The investigator remembers feeling powerless to help, but she told the cleaner, "We can find a lot of help for this. Don't be scared."

Truthfully, Márquez had no idea what she could do. The investigator called Anel Flores, one of her co-workers who was an attorney, to ask for help. Flores suggested that Márquez bring Hernández to their office.

There Hernández was still unable to unearth the words to explain why she was so upset. She could only manage to repeat over and over again that something terrible had happened. "Something was happening, you could see it, but she was crying and she couldn't speak," Flores recalls.

Flores took Hernández into a conference room and closed the door. "There's something going on," she said gently to the janitor.

"Why don't you tell me what's going on so we can figure out what to do?"

Hernández continued to cry without speaking. "Just tell me what you want to tell me, and we'll start from there," Flores said.

For the next two hours, Hernández shared snippets of what had happened at work until Flores was able to piece the whole story together, from the rape in the parking lot to the coerced sex in the motel. Finally Hernández told Flores that she was pregnant from one of the rapes. She was still holding a paper she had received from a health clinic confirming the pregnancy test results.

The janitor had already made an appointment for an abortion. "I cannot have this baby," she told Flores.

Hernández added that she was worried people would find out that she was pregnant, and that she would be judged and blamed for everything that had happened. Flores tried to reassure her: "It's not your fault. You did not do anything wrong. You did not do anything to cause this. You're not a bad person."

But it was clear from her despair that Hernández did not believe it.

Hernández eventually agreed to let Flores share some of what had happened to her with Márquez and Lilia García, the executive director of the Maintenance Cooperation Trust Fund. The three worker advocates told Hernández that they would help her address the problem step by step, in the ways that the cleaner felt would be the most comfortable. They became her confidants and a support network dedicated to helping her out of crisis.

When Hernández terminated the pregnancy a few days later, Flores picked her up from the clinic and delivered her home. After an attorney specializing in sexual harassment suggested that Hernández file a police report, Flores and Márquez drove Hernández to the police station, and Flores sat with her as she was interviewed.

Feeling reassured by the support of the women from the

Maintenance Cooperation Trust Fund, Hernández became determined to push back against what had happened. With the help of the lawyer she had met through the organization, Hernández filed a sexual harassment lawsuit against the cleaning company. In the legal filing, Hernández accused the company of failure to prevent sexual harassment, wrongful termination and retaliation, negligent supervision, intentional infliction of emotional distress, and assault and battery. Within months, the company paid a financial settlement to close the case, though it did not admit any liability in the process. It also fired the supervisor.[2]

Hernández says the outcome of the case can never make up for the rapes, but she is proud that she set aside her fears to challenge what had happened to her. She had tolerated too much for too long because she didn't know how to get help, and she might have been stuck with the same problems if Márquez hadn't found her at work, cleaning the movie theater. "I would have guarded all of this pain," she says. "I wouldn't have known how to speak out about what happened.

"If I had known Vicky from the beginning, I would not have suffered the harassment, the things that happened to me," Hernández says. "When I met Vicky, I stopped saying that I was going to continue to suffer, that I would continue to endure and continue without the ability to say no. All those other times, I was afraid to lose my job."

The experience transformed Hernández. She became diligent in tracking her hours and her rest breaks, and proactive about advising other workers about their rights. "What gives me strength now is that I know my rights in this country," she says. "Even if I'm undocumented, now I know that there are laws that can help us and defend our rights."

Márquez says the isolation of the job and the demographic of the workers makes night-shift cleaners like Hernández easy targets for abuse. "It's because the supervisors always think that the worker needs work and they have work to give," Márquez says. "So they commit these abuses. And there are many—who knows how many hundreds or thousands of cases—that remain in the shadows because no one knows. Many women don't say anything out of fear. They're afraid that society will realize that they have been forced to sleep with someone. They are afraid that they will lose their job."

Márquez knows that it is rare to uncover cases like Hernández's. She and her co-workers are making random nighttime visits to buildings that are being cleaned when few others are around. For each building, there are hundreds more. For each janitor they reach, it can take months of calls and visits before a worker will begin to think about speaking up about the problems. For taboo topics like sexual assault, it takes even more work and time to expose the problem. "How many cases are there in this country that we don't know about?" Márquez says. "Because no one is there investigating. Because we cannot reach them. When I saw this case of harassment, I said, 'My God, there need to be many investigators looking into the many places where this can happen.'"

Sexual assault can happen to anyone, anywhere, but if there is a perfect storm of factors that put workers at risk, night-shift janitorial work is at its epicenter.[3] Nearly every office building in America relies on janitors, but we rarely see the people who do the vacuuming and mopping. The work is scheduled to happen at night or during the early morning, when few people are around. They are expected to be invisible.

Janitorial work is also emblematic of a larger trend toward subcontracting that makes it easier to paper over problems on the job.[4] Before the 1980s, most businesses and stores had their own janitorial staff. Then as institutional investors purchased high-rises to build out their real estate portfolios and retailers grew into chains with locations all over the country, it became more efficient to outsource janitorial work to contractors to minimize cost and liability.

The industry has become even more diffuse and mysterious with the rise in subcontracting. While one contractor might land the official cleaning contract with a big-box store or big city high-rise, it might hire a subcontractor to do the actual cleaning. Some of the subcontractors might then subcontract some or all of the work to a third business. The hazy web of bosses and employers makes it easier for labor abuses to go undetected.

This system has not resulted in healthy salaries and work conditions for cleaners. Building owners, retailers, and businesses award contracts to the lowest bidder, so cleaning companies—both big corporations and mom-and-pop subcontractors—have to keep costs as low as possible. Human labor is the largest expense in this business, and it is where cleaning companies look first to trim costs. According to what is reported to the government, janitors earn about $27,000 a year.[5] The reality is often quite different.

Labor advocates say that the lowest-bidder system means that it is easy—even necessary—to exploit janitors. "The way you make money in this industry is to cheat, because the profit margin is so thin," says Stephen Lerner, who in the 1980s led the Justice for Janitors campaign, the first national effort after World War II to organize cleaners by the Service Employees International Union (SEIU).[6]

Lerner says that there are a number of unseemly strategies a contractor might use to win a contract. They might promise a client that an unrealistic amount of work will be done during a shift, knowing that their staff will have to work longer hours without additional pay to finish it—the very scenario that Hernández experienced. Janitors might be forced to clock in using two different names to avoid racking up overtime. Or unscrupulous contractors might call their employees independent contractors to avoid adhering to labor laws.

Janitorial work is in many ways primed for exploitation, and the people who gravitate toward this work are also not inclined to make complaints about it. It is an industry that takes all comers, and those who seek out the tough and thankless work usually have few options. Some are undocumented, and others lack the formal education or language skills to land other jobs. When workers feel compelled to keep a job at any cost, it reinforces a power dynamic that makes them easier to abuse.

Then there is the simple fact that the job keeps workers hidden and separated. Night-shift janitors fan out in small teams to anonymous buildings every night. The isolation of the work and the fact that the workers are spread out over entire cities makes it hard to track what is really happening.

In the 1980s and 1990s, the SEIU tried to confront these conditions with its Justice for Janitors campaign. The union realized that traditional methods of organizing—convincing workers at a particular job site to vote for union representation—wasn't going to work when janitors working for the same company were dispersed throughout a single city.

The union was also grappling with the fact that the janitorial workforce was changing. Through the 1970s, the industry was made up primarily of African American workers, but as janitorial salaries and unionized jobs declined—non-unionized cleaners might have made $3.40 an hour in 1988—Latino immigrants from Mexico and Central America began to fill the jobs. And increasingly, the work was done by women—today 34 percent of building maintenance workers are female. The union had to find ways to reach a new demographic in a new language.

With activists like Stephen Lerner at the helm, the union decided to organize the industry as a whole instead of focusing on individual work sites. It also decided to target the people who they believed had the power to improve conditions: the building owners who controlled the cleaning contracts, not the janitorial contractors, who were often at the mercy of the low-bid process.

Public shaming became the central strategy. The SEIU staged

noisy protests outside of buildings that paid their janitors too little. They mounted political theater at fine-dining restaurants and golf clubs frequented by targeted real estate moguls. The union made public how much a real estate company earned in profits in comparison to the people cleaning the buildings they owned. Street protests, like a 1990 march from Beverly Hills to Century City in Los Angeles, also helped galvanize public support for janitors, especially when the police unnecessarily attacked a group of participants that included children and pregnant women.

These in-your-face strategies worked. In cities like Los Angeles and Philadelphia, most cleaning contracts for big high rises—regardless of which cleaning company was hired to do the work—stipulated decent baseline pay and healthier working conditions.

However, in the decades since, the split between unionized and non-unionized janitors has deepened. A unionized company can still subcontract to a non-unionized one. And retailers and big-box stores have largely avoided signing union contracts for janitorial work. As an industry that doesn't tend to get much attention from the government or the public, it functions without scrutiny.

It is also an industry that is relatively opaque. The largest corporations are easiest to track, and they provide regular paychecks and benefits to workers. It is easy to recognize janitors working for these larger firms at airports, shopping malls, and government buildings by their clearly marked uniforms. Workers for these bigger-name outfits still have their grievances about wages and sexual harassment, judging by the lawsuits filed against these companies in courts throughout the country. But at least these companies respond to lawsuits and are in a position to seek solutions to the problem.

At the other end of the spectrum are the unknown number of black-market subcontractors that, either out of ignorance or intent to violate the law, never bother to register with the government as official businesses. They may be little mom-and-pop companies operating on a shoestring, or they may be criminal enterprises that use anonymity as a way to skirt the law. In an industry this diffuse and invisible, it's hard to tell these types apart, and when problems arise, the misconduct stays hidden.

This is the black vortex that Lilia García tries to wrangle under control as the director of the Maintenance Cooperation Trust Fund. A native of East Los Angeles, García is a forceful presence with a big laugh.

She says she's predisposed to align herself with the workers her organization seeks out. Her parents immigrated from Mexico, and when they arrived in the United States, her mother took a job as a garment worker. Her father worked up to three jobs to put García and her siblings through college.

García has seen countless examples of janitors who work for a month and then get stiffed on their paychecks. She has handled cases where bosses harangue workers or threaten them with violence for refusing to work without pay or for trying to exercise their rights. She says one supervisor from Los Angeles not only failed to pay his employees what they were due, but he would also lay a gun on the table to remind them who was in charge when cleaners came to pick up their meager paychecks.

García saw that it was unlikely that night-shift janitors would be able to make it to her office just south of downtown Los Angeles to make a complaint in their free time. The only way to find out what was really happening was to be on the ground. She hired field investigators like Vicky Márquez, former janitors or immigrants who are relatable to the workers, so they could meet the cleaners where they already were—on the night shift. This makes her group almost singular in its efforts, and California's labor commissioner often relies on García's group to turn up cases.

"Everywhere you have a physical structure, you have a janitor," García says from her office, where family photos share wall space with political posters. "We really want to make sure that they understand that they have rights. If they have any questions about their working conditions, we're a resource for them."

In many ways, García's team is doing what the government could be doing, though the state and federal departments of labor rarely do night-shift outreach. "The reality is that there are very few or no enforcement agencies who do this work," García says. The cases that her organization brings would otherwise be unreported.

When it comes to sexual violence cases like Hernández's, labor agencies are almost silent on the subject. In states like California, there is a push to create regulations around workplace violence that would address everything from physical attacks to sexual assault. At the federal level, the U.S. Occupational Safety and Health Administration (OSHA) acknowledges that it has a responsibility to address sexual assault on the job, and the federal government estimates that fifty people are sexually assaulted or raped at work every day.[7] In reality, though, OSHA doesn't do much to tackle the issue. It took on its first case of workplace sexual assault in 2016.[8]

It is up to García and her investigators to do the tough work of finding the hardest cases that no one else is looking for. "There is not a presence in these work sites of hotline numbers, of where to call if you're in trouble, of what you can do if a right is violated or if you're attacked," García says. "They were almost like these lost islands just operating in the middle of the night for years and years and years. We're actually connecting them with society and letting them know that their working conditions are wrong or that an attack on their person was wrong and there's something that they can do about it."

These cases rarely come to public attention. On the rare occasions when sexual abuse at work does come to light, it is easy to bury and hide from wider view.

On-the-job sexual assault is both a crime and an extreme form of sexual harassment, a type of workplace discrimination outlawed by the Civil Rights Act of 1964. Nevertheless, companies do not have to disclose how many sexual harassment complaints they receive internally, whether the claims were physical and violent, or how they handled them.

Complaints made to government agencies are often kept confidential until one party decides to file a lawsuit. Less than 1 percent of the sexual harassment complaints the federal government receives result in litigation.[9] The rest are processed and then stored in filing cabinets or databases.

Even lawsuits don't always reveal much about what is really happening. If a worker threatens to file a sexual harassment lawsuit, the company can buy the person's silence by offering a confidential settlement before the case is filed and becomes public information. Cases that do make it to the courthouse can be kept under wraps through quick settlement agreements that include confidentiality clauses that silence the worker and sometimes their attorneys about the claims.

Of course, some workers don't want their personal business to be known to everyone. Meanwhile, companies argue that keeping these claims out of the public eye is necessary. They say that they settle cases as a way to end an embarrassing complaint, even when they don't truly believe the harassment happened. As a result, they worry that these lawsuits can sometimes become a kind of extortion by disgruntled or dishonest employees.

Worker advocates like Lilia García, however, argue that it's difficult enough to convince janitors to come forward about non-taboo job problems like being paid less than the minimum wage. On the dozens of occasions where her organization has unearthed cases involving sexual violence, the abused workers, for the most part, haven't wanted to move forward with formal complaints because they didn't want anyone to know what had happened.

"Most of the victims, it's very internalized," García says. "They internalize the shame and the wrongdoing, and the amount of embarrassment is just overpowering. They choose not to talk about this to any of their relatives. They really have no other support outside of whatever our organization can provide.

"We're talking about workers that are earning, overall, a lower wage if it's not a poverty wage," she adds. "We're talking about people who tend to be in crisis. Their home lives tend to be a challenge. Their child-rearing tends to be a challenge. They're coming to the workplace with a lot of issues. I think all of those factors combine. Unfortunately, it's why, in the janitorial industry, we have such a tremendous amount of unreported sexual crimes."

It is not just night-shift janitors who are at risk for workplace sexual assault. There are other unseen low-wage industries, like farm work and domestic work, done by people who are routinely ignored in places where no one is actively looking. These jobs share similar risk factors. Workers find themselves in isolated work environments during late night or early morning hours, and because they are battling poverty, they are eager to do what it takes to keep their jobs.

Throughout the country, labor enforcement is predicated on the idea that workers already know their rights, and thus it's logical to expect them to make a complaint to bosses or the government if problems arise. These laws don't take into consideration the experiences of low-wage immigrant workers and what their options really look like if they've been sexually assaulted at work.

When sexual assault happens among invisible workers in industries that few are monitoring, it becomes a crime that can be denied, a problem that never receives accountability or prevention. The repercussions of ignoring the realities of vulnerable workers are clear: If on-the-job sexual violence rarely comes to light, then the problem goes unaddressed and the perpetrator is free to abuse again.

"At this point, nine out of ten times, no one complains, or the company covers for you," García says. "There's no accountability. The behavior's not going to stop."

The Maintenance Cooperation Trust Fund does what it can with its team of undercover investigators in California. There are groups in Minneapolis and Boston that do similar work among janitors. But given all of the buildings that are cleaned every night throughout the country, there aren't nearly enough Vicky Márquezes looking for workers who can expose what is really going on during the night shift.

2

The Open Secret

On one of the long days of Eastern Washington's apple harvest in 2004, Norma Valdez was inspecting a bin of just-picked fruit when she heard the foreman's pickup truck approaching. She knew she had to move quickly. She tucked herself between two apple trees, hoping that the leafy branches would obscure her as he drove past.

Valdez had begun to hide from the foreman, Juan Marín, she says, after he attacked her in his truck. A single mother, Valdez couldn't afford to give up her job, so as a kind of self-defense strategy, she had started to find ways to avoid him.

On that particular fall day, she leaned against an apple tree, silent and tensed between the branches. When she was sure Marín was gone, she turned to resume her work. But she had been wrong. Marín had found her and he wanted to know why she had been hiding. Before she could answer, she says, he pinned her against a tree as he grabbed at her breasts and her body. She says he tried to kiss her, and she could feel his saliva on her face. She pushed him away and tried to fight him. Finally, at the height of her panic, he let her go and walked away.

Valdez was not Marín's only target. Over the years, other female farmworkers working under the orchard foreman said that he had abused his power and used the conditions of agricultural work to his advantage. Their stories of sexual harassment and assault took on a recognizable pattern.[1]

Magdalena Álvarez said that in 2008 she had been attacked in Marín's truck after he told her she was needed in another part of the orchard. She had screamed and fought him until he agreed to take her back to the main worksite.

In 2009, a woman named Esther Abarca said that Marín had taken her to an isolated part of the orchard in his truck, where he tried to take off her pants and shirt. She screamed and cried until he relented, and then he offered her money to keep quiet about what had happened.

Going as far back as 1993, a fifteen-year-old named María Lopes called the police to accuse Marín of assaulting her in his pickup. According to the sheriff's report, Lopes had fallen off a ladder while picking apples, and Marín offered to drive her home. After she got in his truck, Marín reached over to touch her injured side, and then moved his hand up to her left breast and squeezed it. "She told him NO and he told her not to be afraid. Mr. Marín placed his hand on her left leg and pulled her zipper down," the report said.

Lopes's case was eventually closed because there had been no witnesses. "At this point it's his word against hers," the deputy sheriff wrote.

Aside from Lopes, none of the other women reported Marín's attacks to the police or to the owners of the orchard directly. The other women said they were too embarrassed to talk about it and they figured that since Marín was their boss, no one would believe them. So for a while, they had all just gotten back to work.

For decades, extreme sexual harassment has been an open secret in the fields. "This has been one of those hazards of the job of being a farmworker because the way that farmworker women are treated, they are looked at as sex objects, actually, when they are out there in the field," says Dolores Huerta, the acclaimed civil rights and labor activist who cofounded the United Farm Workers with César Chávez.

To navigate this reality, strategies for avoiding danger and protecting oneself are passed around among female workers, who make up about 25 percent of the agricultural labor force. Women in the fields cover their faces with bandanas and tie sweatshirts around their waists, even in the hottest weather, to thwart the male gaze. Like Norma Valdez, they avoid violent advances by hiding from problem co-workers or working near trusted ones. Because single women are considered easy targets, some female farmworkers lie about their home life and pretend to have husbands and boyfriends when they don't.

The fact that female farmworkers routinely suffer from extreme sexual harassment first came to wider attention when the Southern Poverty Law Center partnered with a variety of organizations in 2007 to launch the "bandana project." Mónica Ramírez, a center staffer at the time, convened farmworker women and community organizations in dozens of cities across the country to decorate bandanas with symbols and stories related to their experiences of sexual harassment in the fields. The bandanas were then displayed in museums, libraries, community centers, and rape crisis centers. A few years later, the center interviewed 150 immigrant women workers in the agricultural industry and published a report about the "enduring near-constant sexual harassment in the fields and factories."[2]

Human Rights Watch followed with another study. The organization interviewed fifty farmworkers and found that female farmworkers "face a real and significant risk of sexual violence and sexual harassment."[3]

Both reports observed that very few women reported these crimes to bosses or law enforcement because there can be real consequences:

Farmworkers who push back against the abuse, or report incidents to management, say they suffer retaliation, getting fewer
hours, more abusive treatment, or, worst of all, losing their
jobs altogether. Because many farmworkers work with family
members, retaliation can mean the victim is fired along with
her family, resulting in loss of income to the entire household.
Those who live in employer-provided housing can even find
themselves homeless. Some farmworkers who had filed sexual harassment lawsuits reported they were "blackballed" and
shut out of jobs at other farms.

The prevalence of sexual harassment and assault in the fields
is incalculable, but these reports have helped elucidate how entrenched the problem has become. A 2010 study of 150 California
farmworkers by a UC Santa Cruz researcher found that 40 percent
of the women said they had been harassed in some way, ranging
from sexual comments to rape.[4] In a survey of 100 meatpacking
plant workers in Iowa by ASISTA, a national advocacy group focused on helping immigrant victims of crime, 41 of the women said
they had experienced unwanted touching at work and 30 said they
had been on the receiving end of sexual propositions. More than a
quarter said their harasser had threatened them with harder work
or losing their jobs if they didn't go along with the harassment.[5]

No survey or study can offer a true tabulation of the problem.
"We have not yet counted those that are not courageous enough
to tell their stories, or all the women that don't know their rights,
and all the women that don't have transportation to come here
and complain," says Jesús López, a community worker in Salinas,
California.

For more than two decades, López has worked for California
Rural Legal Assistance (CRLA), an organization that has been on
the front lines of representing farmworkers with almost any kind of

problem, including workplace sexual assault. A man of sturdy build and jovial character, López has earned a reputation for solving the intense but prosaic problems that immigrants living in rural California can face. A native of Mexico, he knows the farmworker life because he spent nearly two decades in the fields himself.

Most weeks, López splits his time between his office on a busy intersection of east Salinas and the farm fields of the Salinas Valley, where he makes sure workers receive enough water and shade as required by state law. When people come to his office looking for help about problems with their paycheck, their housing conditions, or issues with pesticide exposure, he is often one of the first people they meet. If they need legal help, he refers them to one of the in-house lawyers. If they need something else—an emergency loan or housing for a few days—he searches for solutions.

López is proud of the trust he's developed in all corners of the Latino community in Salinas, but it means his life and work often blend together. He gives out his cell phone number without hesitation, and it rings constantly, even on evenings when he is having dinner with his wife or playing guitar in the church band.

In 1996, it was not out of the ordinary when a farmworker named Blanca Alfaro came to California Rural Legal Assistance asking specifically to see López. The first couple of times she stopped in, López was out in the fields, but Alfaro was persistent. After two weeks of trying, López and Alfaro had their first meeting in his office.

Almost immediately, López could tell that Alfaro was upset. But when he asked her what kind of help she needed, she insisted that the only thing that was wrong was that the lettuce farm that had fired her owed her $34 in wages.

López knew something else was bothering her.

It was only after some patient prodding that Alfaro opened up about the other problem she had been dealing with: Her supervisor demanded sex in exchange for a job every season. Her boyfriend, who worked at the same lettuce farm, had recently been fired after he complained to management about the supervisor.

Alfaro's reluctance to discuss the harassment is a pattern López has seen again and again. "No one comes here to say, 'I have been harassed,'" López says. "They always come saying, 'I am here because I was unjustly fired. I am here because I didn't get my pay. I am here because the *mayordomo* [foreman] is mistreating me.'"

López says he's come to understand that when workers initially come to make a sexual harassment complaint, it's to salvage their livelihood, not necessarily to seek justice through the legal system. "I am seeing a violation of the law and they are seeing an economic situation and I did not understand that," he says. "They knew that it was very likely that they could lose their jobs and not make the rent anymore."

The lawyers in his office were ready to help Alfaro, but as the community worker who would help shepherd the farmworker through the process, López knew he needed to better understand the problem. That fall, he signed up for a training program offered by the U.S. Equal Employment Opportunity Commission, the federal government entity that polices on-the-job sexual harassment.

When he got there, he met an investigator for the commission and they got to talking. López began to tell the investigator about Alfaro's case; she took what López had told her to her boss, William R. Tamayo, then a regional attorney for the commission based in San Francisco. After Alfaro filed a formal complaint against the company, Tamayo's office took on the case.

Tamayo says that when López approached the commission with the Alfaro case, farmworker sexual assault was a problem that was beginning to come to the fore in his office, which oversees much of the Western United States. A number of farmworker advocates at the time had begun to urge the agency to look into these cases.

"They said farmworker women were talking about the fields as the *fils de calzón,* or fields of panties," he says. "They referred to the fields as the 'green motel.'"

After investigating Alfaro's case, the federal commission eventually filed a sexual harassment lawsuit against Tanimura & Antle, the lettuce grower that had employed Alfaro, for failing to protect her from her supervisor's assaults. This became the commission's first lawsuit against a major agricultural employer, and the case settled for more than $1.8 million in 1999.[6] Though the company did not admit wrongdoing, it was required through the settlement to offer sexual harassment training to its workers.

The U.S. Equal Employment Opportunity Commission has the authority to tackle rape and sexual assault in the fields because it upholds Title VII, the section of the federal Civil Rights Act of 1964 that protects workers from discrimination on the job. Under the law, severe and persistent workplace sexual harassment—whether verbal or physical—is illegal because it's considered a kind of gender-based discrimination.

Using civil rights laws to address sexual violence at work may seem counterintuitive, but it has been the most clear-cut path to redress for many workers. The U.S. Equal Employment Opportunity Commission is charged with investigating worker complaints and then making a determination about whether there is evidence of good cause. For sexual harassment cases, the commission tends to find reasonable cause in about half of the complaints it receives.

For cases the commission decides to take on, it often pursues reforms and financial settlements with employers by facilitating a mediation process. If the company and its employees cannot come to a solution out of court, the commission files a civil lawsuit. At that point, the complaint against the company becomes public.

The weight of the federal commission is significant, and lawyers who represent companies big and small say that this style of government enforcement makes businesses feel strong-armed into making payouts and concessions even when it is not clear that they have done anything wrong.[7]

Mary Schultz is a Washington-based lawyer who represents workers, though she once spent months defending ABM Industries, a major facility services provider, in a Minnesota sexual harassment case. She says the experience of representing a corporation helped her see firsthand why companies feel compelled to fight sexual harassment and other lawsuits related to on-the-job problems. "Do companies just start opening the wallet, paying out money to people whose circumstances they believe?" she asks. "I think that would be horribly risky for any company. You would end up getting complaints from every angle, you would end up with varying motivations for complaints. You would be overwhelmed with trying to sort out the good from the bad."

Employers certainly can't be expected to single-handedly prevent all cases of sexual harassment, so standards have been established through case law about when a business is at fault and when it is not. Generally speaking, companies are liable for sexual harassment only if they fail to respond to complaints once they become aware of them. "The law is clear that you have to fix the problem," says Stephen Hirschfeld, an attorney who represents employers in sexual harassment cases. "How you do it is up to you."

Employers can also avoid legal liability if they show that the victim was being unreasonable by not bringing the problem to the company's attention. Alternately, employers can argue that the harassment didn't happen at all, or that the offending behavior doesn't meet the legal standard of having been "severe or pervasive."

That the government is suing companies and not always the perpetrators of the sexual harassment or assault is one of the limitations of civil lawsuits—these cases often turn into tussles over seemingly mundane questions about legal liability.

Mary Schultz, the Washington employment attorney, says that

these legal arguments over liability can sometimes feel divorced from the actual allegations of sexual harassment. The questions start to center on technical issues, such as whether the plaintiff is suing the right business entity or whether the company was on notice about the harassment. "In court, the arguments are, in large part, technical and perhaps less about what actually happened," she says. "The law is the law. There are elements that have to be proven. Some of that has little to do with what actually happened."

Despite their inherent constraints, civil lawsuits have become one of the few ways that sexually abused workers can seek recourse. And from the government's point of view, these cases can have systemwide or industrywide impacts. In its settlement agreements with companies, the U.S. Equal Employment Opportunity Commission generally requires that they make improvements to how sexual harassment is handled. "We seek what we call injunctive relief, relief that looks for a remedy to what we feel was a violation that led us to sue them in the first place," says Anna Park, a regional attorney for the commission.

Since the Alfaro case, the commission has prioritized cases on behalf of low-income and immigrant workers like farmworkers, janitors and other vulnerable and underserved laborers. When it comes to farm work, it has filed more than forty sexual harassment lawsuits against agricultural companies in the past fifteen years, and the allegations tend to involve extreme claims like rape and sexual assault.

This docket of lawsuits hints at the severe nature of the harassment experienced by agricultural workers, and the incidents span the map. In Iowa, female workers at DeCoster Farms, an egg and poultry processing plant, reported being raped and sexually assaulted by supervisors. The case, which turned up allegations of widespread sexual abuse, was settled in 2002 for about $1.5 million.[8] The company did not admit wrongdoing in the process. In Florida, five women working at a packing plant for Moreno Farms said that they had been raped or sexually harassed by three male supervisors. The owners of the farm never responded to the lawsuit so the women won their case by default. A jury later awarded the workers more than $17 million in 2015.[9]

Back in California, a farmworker named Olivia Tamayo (who is not related to the federal commission's William R. Tamayo) pressed her civil sexual harassment case to trial in 2004. She worked for Harris Farms, one of the largest agribusinesses in the country, and she said that in 1993, she was raped by a supervisor named René Rodríguez in his truck while his gun rested on the dashboard. She said the supervisor raped her a second time later that year and then again in 1994, and both times, he carried a gun. Tamayo also testified that she feared Rodríguez, so for years, she didn't tell anyone about the rapes, not even her husband.

After a twenty-three-day trial, a jury found in favor of Tamayo and awarded her nearly $1 million.[10] The company appealed the judgment but the higher court affirmed the decision in Tamayo's favor.[11]

The lawsuit did not convince the company that it or Rodríguez had done anything wrong. Representatives of the company have also maintained that any sex between Tamayo and Rodríguez was consensual, and they allowed him to retire in 1999.

Joe Del Bosque, a Central Valley grower and a past president of the farmworker safety organization AgSafe, says that for employers, claims like Olivia Tamayo's are hard to sort out. "The trouble with a lot of sexual harassment cases is that it's one person's word against the other person's word and who do you believe?" he says. "I know that doesn't make any of that all right but those are always very difficult cases."

Nevertheless, he says the Tamayo case put everyone in the area on notice. "That caught a lot of farmers' attention—a lot of employers' attention—that they could be liable for huge sums of money if there was a case of sexual harassment brought against them," Del Bosque says.

In 2006, sexual harassment complaints about a Yakima Valley apple orchard foreman named Juan Marín began to surface. Marín was working for Evans Fruit, one of the largest apple producers in the country. The family-run business is known in Eastern Washington as a solid and steady employer that hires hundreds of seasonal workers year-round for tasks ranging from picking apples to thinning fruit trees. Built through grit and sacrifice by husband and wife Bill and Jeannette Evans, the company has an all-American creation story to match its down-to-earth owners, who met as teenagers at a local chocolate shop.

The couple built its impressive apple empire starting with just a ten-acre parcel of land. Today, the scale of the operation is massive, and Evans Fruit harvests apples from nine thousand acres spread across eleven orchards spanning the Yakima Valley. To get from one ranch to another can take almost an hour by car.

The Evans's second-largest orchard is in Sunnyside, Washington, a 1,700-acre property fifty miles from the Evans Fruit headquarters in Cowiche. For decades, Juan Marín presided over the day-to-day operation in Sunnyside as orchard foreman. His Horatio Alger–style rise within Evans Fruit is something to marvel at. In the 1970s, as a teenager, he says he sneaked into the United States through Tijuana crammed in the back of a truck, where he and others were packed as tightly as cigarettes. Once he made it across the border, Marín kept heading north until he landed a job in an apple orchard in Washington, and he started his career with Evans Fruit, digging out rocks in the fields so that trees could be planted in the orchards. With a capacity for exceptional industry, he impressed Bill and Jeannette Evans with his work ethic, and he was eventually asked to manage the Sunnyside ranch in 1981.

There he was responsible for hiring and overseeing more than five hundred seasonal farmworkers each year. He says he made himself available around the clock, whether it was to transport crates of bees for orchard pollination or to turn on the windmills on cold nights to keep warm air circulating in the orchards. He also became a crucial link between management and workers because of his good, if choppy, English. For all this work, he was paid a salary of $50,000 a year, plus a house rent-free on the orchard and two pickup trucks.

Marín was even able to transcend the trappings of illegal immigration when he married an American citizen, and the couple had two kids together, but the relationship didn't last. He built a new life with an apple picker he met at Evans Fruit. The couple has been together for more than three decades, and they have seven children. Together, they constructed a small real estate empire, and have owned about $2 million in apartment buildings and houses in Sunnyside. Many of their tenants are also employees whom Marín oversaw at Evans Fruit.

Though he was trusted at headquarters, Marín was feared and despised in the orchard. To hear workers talk about it, the Sunnyside ranch had become his fiefdom. Charged with filling hundreds of seasonal jobs in a community hungry for work, he had quite a bit of power to wield.

Workers said he abused his authority, charging kickbacks for jobs at Evans Fruit or collecting utility payments for company housing and then apparently pocketing the cash. He also had a reputation for condoning a sexualized workplace. Some workers said that he personally harassed both the men and women who worked for him, and that there was a remote place in the orchard that he called La Joyita, or The Little Jewel, where he supposedly took women for sex.

To the workers, Marín seemed untouchable because he gave off the impression that owners Bill and Jeannette Evans treated him like a son, which the couple has denied. But in the orchards of the Sunnyside ranch, Marín's word held undue weight.

The rumors about sexual harassment in the Sunnyside orchards had circulated for decades, but the silence was finally broken by seventeen-year-old Jacqueline Abundez, who took a summer job with her mother and brother at Evans Fruit in 2006.

Abundez and her family, like many of the company's employees, were relative newcomers to the Yakima Valley, part of the latest wave of Mexican immigrants who had come to work in the busy apple, cherry, and hop orchards. Abundez lived in a crowded house at the end of an unpaved street not far from the Sunnyside ranch, where the median household income hovers around $34,000.

Abundez's mother, Ángela Mendoza, supported her family through apple picking because it was work she could manage with no English and little formal education. A stout and fiery woman with blazing green eyes, Mendoza had worked at Evans Fruit for several seasons and when she brought her children with her that summer for work, she expected to pick fruit alongside them. On their first day of work that summer, however, Juan Marín separated them into different areas, which made Mendoza nervous.

Mendoza was familiar with the rumors about Marín, so she demanded that the foreman let her daughter work near her. He agreed. Still, Mendoza says, it didn't shield her daughter from Marín's advances. She says she was horrified when he came up behind Abundez and snuggled up against her. When Mendoza tried to intervene by telling him to treat his workers with respect, she said the foreman laughed at her.

Mendoza says Marín also said vulgar things to her about her daughter, such as asking her for Abundez's hand in marriage. "Give me your daughter," Mendoza recalls him saying. "I'll have her give birth to a child year after year."

Disgusted but uncowed, Mendoza took her concerns to the U.S. Equal Employment Opportunity Commission, where both she and

Abundez filed a complaint against the company based on Marín's behavior. Neither of them had gone to the company directly with their complaints, so Evans Fruit first got notice about the problem from the federal commission. In response, Bill and Jeannette's son, Tim Evans, paid Marín a visit. He asked the orchard foreman whether he had harassed Abundez, and Marín denied it. He also spoke to two crew leaders, who backed up Marín's denial.[12] Nevertheless, Tim Evans told Marín that he could no longer give anyone rides in his truck, and Bill Evans followed up by sending Marín a warning letter: "This is the second time this year that we have received a complaint about your conduct from the Equal Employment Opportunity Commission. We don't have the time or energy to continue dealing with the problems you are bringing down on us. Any further incidents or complaints of sexual harassment and you will be discharged."

The letter was an empty warning. Less than a year later, Marín was the subject of another sexual harassment complaint when Wendy Granados, an apple picker, filed a claim with the federal government that said the foreman regularly offered women raises, cars, and houses for sexual favors.

The complaints continued. At headquarters, the Evanses received an anonymous letter complaining about Marín, including his penchant for sexual harassment. Months later, in 2008, the company received a fourth sexual harassment complaint from the federal commission. This time, it was filed by Norma Valdez, the apple checker who said she had been attacked by Marín in his truck and then had started hiding from him.

Marín denied all of the sexual harassment complaints against him to the company and continues to deny the allegations to anyone who asks. "I never bother nobody," he says. "The only thing I've been doing in my life is work. I'm so upset because it's a bunch of rumors, a bunch of lies. There's nothing true."

Because there was no physical evidence of sexual harassment—it was numerous female workers' complaints against the word of one longtime male employee—Evans Fruit let the foreman keep his job.

The lawsuit that emerged from the sexual harassment complaints against Juan Marín illustrates just how difficult it can be to decide who should have done what—and when—in response to a complaint of sexual violence at work. Employers are sometimes left to parse shocking accusations against trusted employees, even as the financial risk that accompanies these claims means companies might give them extra credence. But in the breakdown of these so-called "he-said, she-said" cases, the stories of men and women don't always carry equal weight.

After the various complaints against Marín came in, the federal commission conducted an investigation, which turned up additional workers who said they had been sexually harassed by Marín or other crew leaders.

One young woman told investigators that she had witnessed and lived through Juan Marín's harassment, but she didn't want to join the lawsuit. The experience still plagues her. On a winter afternoon a few years ago, she drove down two-lane Chaffee Road, a few miles from the Sunnyside orchard, to point out the house that she said Marín had offered her in exchange for sleeping with him. She still trembles at the thought of the foreman, and even after all of these years, she is horrified by the harassment.

Marín had been persistent in his sexual advances, so she didn't stay on the job for long. She found work at a Mexican restaurant, where she waited tables seven days a week and nurtured dreams of going to community college. She said she didn't participate in the lawsuit or want her name used because she hadn't told her family about what had happened at Evans Fruit. Maybe she never would.

In 2010, after efforts between Evans Fruit and its employees to resolve the case privately didn't work out, the government filed a lawsuit against the company. Other crew leaders and male workers at Evans Fruit were accused of sexual harassment, but Marín remained at the center of the claims. The Northwest Justice Project, a legal aid organization, stepped in to represent some of the women in the federal case and to help three of them file their own claims in state court.

In court filings, the government and the workers claimed that the company failed to prevent the sexual harassment the women had experienced. The company countered that the women had unreasonably failed to complain to the company about the problem but that once it had been notified of the initial claims, it had done a prompt and thorough investigation.

As the case moved through the legal system, Marín's carefully constructed world collapsed. He had managed to fend off the sexual harassment accusations for a while, but in 2010, Bill Evans fired him and stripped him of his duties and his title—but not because of the sexual harassment complaints.

In the process of fighting the lawsuit, the Evanses had started to do some digging. They discovered that Marín had stolen an unknown amount of money from the company—one estimate put it at about $500,000—by setting up fake or "ghost" employees at Evans Fruit. He'd kept for himself the money issued to these nonexistent workers. The company also found that Marín had assigned orchard employees to work on his rental apartments during company time.

While there are suspicions that the embezzled money is what allowed Marín and his wife to buy millions of dollars in real estate on a $50,000 salary, Marín insists that he has never stolen from his employer. "I was the best foreman," Marín says. "I send the best fruit to the warehouse. I'm so upset with Evans Fruit because they didn't believe me."

Dethroned, he was forced to take odd jobs around town. In 2013, a few months before the government's lawsuit against Evans Fruit was set to go to trial, Marín stood among a small grove of cherry trees in Zillah, Washington.

"I'm getting blamed for something I never did," he said from atop the ladder, shears in hand. In the filtered winter light, he searched expertly for the sweet spots of the branch to cut away as he talked. "So much bad stuff happened and it's not me. The ones who did the bad stuff are still there. I didn't do nothing."

Later that day, he sat at a park bench and complained that the sexual harassment and assault claims against him had been made by "nasty women" at the behest of his brother and cousin, who he says have a personal vendetta against him. "They're a bunch of liars and a bunch of jealous peoples," he said. "And they're wanting something for nothing. Because I work all the time. And I got a good wife and kids and a good family. I save my money. And they don't."

He went down the list of all of the lawyers involved in the cases against him and said he hoped they would all be fired. He added that he plans to take everyone who made allegations against him to court. "They gonna find out what suffer is," he said.

It had been a clear winter day, and earlier, when Marín had stood at the top of an aluminum ladder to make forceful cuts to the naked branches, the length of the Yakima Valley had opened up around him.

To the north were the cities of Cowiche and Tieton, small farming towns rich with hopyards, pastures, and tightly ordered orchards. To the south was Sunnyside, pungent with animal feedlots, where apples and grapes grew up to the foot of the Rattlesnake Hills.

The upper and lower valleys span more than fifty miles, but the distances within the population—in language, lifestyle, economics, and opportunity—is incalculable. It is a place where the ways that America misunderstands itself racially and economically play out in a kind of quotidian theater. These misconceptions would prove to be one of Marín's greatest allies in the lawsuits filed against him.

In the Sunnyside flats and the surrounding swath of Indian

reservation, there is a pocket where the American Dream dims. It is where little-to-no education meets little-to-no English meets a lack of immigration papers. Houses are packed with extended family, friends, or anyone who can help chip in for rent. Here immigrants and their kids go to work before the sun rises to pick or pack apples or tend to the orchards. In its monotonous physical routine, poverty begins to feel inevitable.

It's an existence that can be hard to fathom from the gated houses high on the hills of Cowiche or further out, in the picturesque towns of Ellensworth and Richland, where longtime locals with jobs at universities or research labs can afford houses in tidy subdivisions. Juan Marín and his accusers came from the Sunnyside flats, but it was the other half of Eastern Washington, that of idyllic values and American-born idealism, that would serve as their judge and jury.

The trial of U.S. *Equal Employment Opportunity Commission v. Evans Fruit* began on March 19, 2013, in the federal courthouse in downtown Yakima. The courtroom held about thirty people, and during eleven days of trial, Bill and Jeannette Evans drove downtown to take front-row seats at the proceeding after early-morning meetings with their staff.

Federal judge Lonny Suko, calm and serious, presided. The jury box had been filled with seven men and two women. They were an all-white and largely Christian group, many of whom said during the selection process that their favorite book was the Bible. One woman said she recognized the judge from church.

Over the course of nearly three weeks, the jury heard from a succession of Evans Fruit employees who were sworn in before taking a seat at the witness stand. Although Ángela Mendoza and her daughter, Jacqueline Abundez, had been the ones to spark the lawsuit, both women were dropped from the case because Abundez was murdered in 2008, and Mendoza's statements about her daughter's sexual harassment claims were now viewed as hearsay. Even so, fourteen additional women testified that Juan Marín or an Evans Fruit crew leader had sexually harassed them. Nearly a half-dozen men also testified that they had observed sexual harassment at the orchard.

When it came to Marín specifically, some of the claimants said that the foreman had propositioned, groped, or sexually assaulted them in the orchard. In his truck, he grabbed their breasts and crotches, tore off their shirts and pulled down their pants, some of them said.

The testimony began to take on a predictable rhythm. The women's lawyers asked them to describe the things that Marín or crew leaders had done to make them feel uncomfortable at work. Some of the workers were asked to stand and show the jury ex-actly where Juan Marín had touched them. The women explained that on top of the shame, embarrassment, and fear of not being believed, they had never reported their problems to the company because they didn't know that they could or because their English was poor. Most of them spoke through an interpreter at trial.

The women were then cross-examined by attorneys representing Evans Fruit, whose mission was to show that the company wasn't liable for any sexual harassment that had happened in the orchards because its managers didn't initially know about it, as the women had never complained to them. The company's lawyers also sought to show that neither Juan Marín nor any of the accused crew lead-ers had the authority to hire or fire seasonal workers, a situation which, if proven, would make it harder to connect the men's behav-ior with the company's legal liability.

In the end, the company's most effective legal strategy was casting doubt on the women's credibility altogether. Lawyers for the company pointed out inconsistencies related to some of the claimants' financial failings and legal missteps. One worker had made a misstatement on a bankruptcy filing. Another had received unemployment checks when she was supposedly working at Evans Fruit. Even some of the government's strongest witnesses were toppled by this type of questioning from Evans Fruit's lawyers.

A case in point was the testimony of Norma Valdez, the woman who had taken to hiding from Marín in the orchard. Petite with blond highlights, Valdez carried herself with an air of maturity and confidence. In the courtroom, she initially won over the jury when one of the government lawyers asked her how she was doing as she took the witness stand and she replied, "Well, nervous but all right." The jurors smiled sympathetically.

Valdez told the jury that she had taken seasonal work at Evans Fruit from 2004 to 2007. She said that she didn't know who Bill and Jeannette Evans were, but she had met their son Tim, who sometimes drove through the orchard in his truck. Since Tim owned his own orchard, she had once asked him for work. The jury also learned that she had been divorced and that her current partner, Gerardo Silva, is someone she met while working at Evans Fruit.

When an attorney for the U.S. Equal Employment Opportunity Commission asked Valdez if orchard foreman Juan Marín had ever done anything that had made her feel uncomfortable, she replied, "Well, there were many."

"The first time he attacked me, that happened in Mattawa, at the Mattawa ranch," she testified. "I was working, and he came to—and, you know, I didn't know he was like that. And he came to—he said he was going to take me to work in a different area, and he said, 'Get in my truck.'"

They drove for some time and Valdez began to get scared, and she asked Marín where they were going. "He said, 'Don't be afraid, don't be afraid,'" Valdez said. "And he continued driving and he took me to the middle of an orchard. He drove his truck in between the rows of apple trees, and he took me far into the field."

He parked the truck and "all of a sudden he was on top of me. He was on top of me, and he was hugging me, touching me, and he was trying to kiss me. And I could feel his saliva on my neck and on my face. And I would push him and push him away so he would let go of me, but he wouldn't," Valdez said. "And I couldn't, you know. I want to get him off me, but I couldn't and . . ."

Where were his hands? "They were all over my body. He was touching my breasts, he was touching me between my legs, he was hugging me until I was finally able to get him off me," she said. "And I opened the door, and I took off running. I took off running and I didn't know where I was at, and he went to catch me. He caught up to me, and he grabbed my arm and he turned me around, and I said, 'If that's why you hired me I'm just going home,' that I was not going to be there if he was going to do that to me."

On the witness stand, Valdez was getting agitated and tearful. "I was shocked," she said. "I didn't know why that had happened. I couldn't understand it."

She told the jury that as time passed, she began to recognize the sound of Marín's truck, and whenever she heard it, she hid from him. She described two more groping incidents in detail and said there had been many more. Though they upset her, she had kept it all to herself. "I was very embarrassed," she said. "It was just embarrassing to tell someone what had happened to me."

Valdez's testimony was convincing, but during her cross-examination, Evans Fruit attorney Carolyn Cairns began with a line of questioning meant to generate doubt about Valdez's veracity: If they had really happened, why didn't she bother to complain?

Cairns insinuated that Valdez should have known how to make a complaint to the company because the farmworker had signed a document when she took the job that said she had received a copy of the company's workplace policies, which said specifically that the Evanses welcomed hearing concerns directly from their workers. The lawyer then asked Valdez why she never complained to Tim Evans, since she had once called him to ask him for a job. Valdez said that she did not think Tim would believe her and that she had been embarrassed. In fact, she hadn't told anyone about what Marín had done to at first, not even her partner, Gerardo Silva.

Cairns saw an opening to further discredit Valdez. She asked her when she had begun her "affair" with Silva. One of the government attorneys objected to the question because it was argumentative and harassing, and Cairns pointed out that Valdez had begun her relationship with Silva while she was still married. The judge asked Cairns to rephrase the question, and the lawyer eventually asked if Valdez had previously said that Marín stopped harassing her after she began dating Silva. Valdez replied that Marín had continued to touch her in ways that she did not like for two more years.

Cairns then returned to the question of why Valdez had never reported the assaults. Why hadn't Valdez gone to the police? Valdez said she didn't know she could. "You knew how to report domestic violence, though, didn't you?" Cairns asked pointedly. Valdez agreed that she had once gone to the police about her ex-husband.

Then Cairns pulled out her trump card. Cairns showed the jury a court document that said that Valdez had pled guilty to welfare fraud in 2002. When asked repeatedly about the particulars, Valdez said she couldn't remember much about what had happened. As persuasive as she had been moments before, Valdez's credibility with the jury was visibly shot.

Although there was a reasonable explanation for the welfare-fraud conviction, Valdez's lawyers weren't able to help her recover. Valdez was only able to tell the jury that she and her ex-husband had filed for welfare when they lived in California because her husband had hurt his hands and couldn't work for a time. Her attorney's effort to elicit more detail was shut down by objections from Evans Fruit's lawyers.

If Valdez had been given an opportunity to more fully explain, the jury would have learned that while she was living in Southern California, Valdez and her then husband had enrolled in welfare after he was injured on the job. Problems arose when the couple agreed to help Valdez's father, who had limited reading and writing skills, buy a car. Her father used the car and made the monthly payments to the dealership, but by signing the title to a second car and not notifying the state government about it, the couple had broken state welfare laws. According to the government complaint against them, the couple had committed a felony because they had "falsely reported that they only owned one car."

At the time, Valdez's husband told government investigators that he had read and signed the forms and "I just have Norma sign them." The couple didn't deny that they held the title for a second car so they pleaded guilty to a misdemeanor. The judge fined them $100, and they each spent one day in the county jail.

There was no way to predict that the incident would be Valdez's undoing in a sexual harassment lawsuit more than a decade later.

Besides raising questions about the women's character, the attorneys for Evans Fruit were also successful at emphasizing the inconsistencies between what the women had said when they had provided sworn pretrial testimony during their depositions and what they said on the witness stand at trial.

It's a common tactic used in civil cases to poke holes in a witness's credibility. Seasoned court watchers know that inconsistencies on the witness stand can happen for a variety of reasons. Sometimes memories falter. In cases involving traumatic events, brain science tells us that victims tend to have a hard time remembering some details or putting them in proper sequence. The way questions are asked—or not asked at all—during the deposition can set the stage for discrepancies later on. A final explanation, which the attorneys for Evans Fruit relied on, was that the witnesses were embellishing or lying.

During trial, several Evans Fruit workers testified about incidents that were never mentioned during their depositions or that had not been included in their initial complaint to the government.

Some of these additions were much more serious than what had been discussed with the company, and they surfaced for the first time at trial. The women later said that they didn't mention some of these incidents earlier because they hadn't been asked about them, but at trial, the company's lawyers argued that the women were fabricating their stories, motivated by the possibility of winning money.

As an Evans Fruit attorney put it at the end of the trial, "The claimants need money and you may consider that that is a powerful incentive to invent or exaggerate their stories. At some level I understand that. These folks are poor. For the most part, they're uneducated, and their career paths, frankly, are not bright. This is their chance to get some extra money, and they're grabbing the brass ring. However sympathetic their financial conditions may be, it is simply not fair and it's not right that they try to get money from Mr. and Mrs. Evans that they do not legally deserve."

The testimony of a worker named Esther Abarca, in particular, illustrated how the women's more detailed and dramatic stories revealed at trial were framed as distortions of the truth. Abarca's testimony was taken on the sixth day of trial, after three women had testified that Juan Marín had sexually harassed them.

Abarca lives in Chicago, and her testimony was given through a live video feed. She wore her hair pulled back and carried a small white handbag. During her testimony, she frequently looked down or cradled her head in her hand or fiddled nervously with the strap of her purse. The camera was trained on her from above, an unflattering angle.

A government lawyer began by asking her about her experience with Juan Marín, and like Norma Valdez, she described an attack in Marín's truck: "I was working like an area where I was topping off, or making bins even, and then Mr. Marín said he was going to move me to another block, to another area," she said. "And he told me to get in his car because I was far—that was far away from there. And at the time I did not have a car of my own. So then I got in, and he took me to a place, he took me to someplace, but at the time I didn't know my way around the ranch very well because I hadn't been there for a long time. I did not know the ranch very well. Then once I was in the car, he was like trying to grab me and I kept telling him that I—to stop, that I didn't like that."

The orchard foreman "came on top of me and he wouldn't let me move, and he was like kissing me and touching me all over," she said. Marín, she said, used the isolation to his advantage:

It was a desolate place. It was there—I was there all alone and, like I said before, I don't know my way around the ranch . . . I wanted to get out and when he got on top of me, he laid me down, on my back in the car. . . . He wanted to remove my clothing. He was able to unbutton my pants, but I kept pushing him away. I told him to leave me alone, that I was with a partner and that I didn't want any problems. . . . He wouldn't let go of me. He wouldn't let go of me, and he wanted to kiss me forcefully. . . . He was touching me all over the place, like this, like from here all the way down. He was grabbing me and touching me all over the place, and he wanted to remove my clothing. He was able to unbutton my pants, but he was only able to pull them down half—halfway down. . . . I kept telling him to leave me alone, but he wouldn't leave me alone. And I kept screaming, but there was nobody there to help because—there was nobody there at that place. . . . After that I started crying out loud and I started screaming to please leave me alone. And after so much crying and screaming he said, "That's it, I'm not going to do anything to you anymore. Get back in the car, I'm going to take you back." . . . Because I was screaming so much and kicking so much and pushing him away so much, he said that he was going to leave me alone finally and that he was going to take me back.

On the video screen, the jury in Yakima watched as Abarca wiped away tears. She said that Marín told her not to tell anyone what had happened and he would give her $3,000 so she could buy a car. "I told him that was the very reason I had come here to work, that I did not need him to give me any money at all," she said.

What had happened in the truck was not the only time Marín had harassed her, Abarca said. At the time, she was living in one of Marín's apartment buildings, and the foreman had assigned her to clean his properties during Evans Fruit work hours. He insisted on driving her there and on the way, she says there was a second attack in Marín's truck. At the rental house she was to clean, she says he assaulted her again. "He cornered me and pinned me against the wall and he tried to pull my pants down again. . . . I had to tell him to leave me alone, to stop, that I didn't want anything to do with him," she said.

She wiped tears from her cheek. She said she did not report these attacks because "I was afraid that I would be fired."

Abarca's testimony had been riveting but as with Norma Valdez, the cross-examination by Evans Fruit attorneys would be her downfall.

Brendan Monahan, an attorney for the company, began by pointing out that in a previous court hearing, Abarca had lied and said that she had not been cleaning Marín's apartments on company time. And, he noted, in her deposition, Abarca had only mentioned that Marín had blown her kisses, called her beautiful and attacked her once in his truck—and now she wanted the jury to believe that there were multiple attacks?

"Yes," she said, "but it is because I was ashamed to say everything and I'm still ashamed now," she said.

Monahan continued to underscore the inconsistencies between Abarca's deposition and what she had told the jury. "And so the story that you're telling the jury today about the apartment and the house and the second incident in the truck, those are new stories, aren't they?" he asked.

On the screen, the jury could see that Abarca was crying. But she was still defiant. "Those are not stories," she retorted. "That's the truth and there is God—if you don't want justice, there's God who knows everything I've been going through."

Monahan, normally unflappable, appeared startled.

After a pause, he made a motion to strike Abarca's statement. The judge agreed, so Abarca's outburst could not be considered as evidence by the jury.

On the eighth day of trial, Juan Marín arrived to testify, dressed in a gray button-down shirt and jeans. His hair, normally kept under control by a baseball cap, had been carefully brushed back. Though he prided himself on being bilingual, he testified in Spanish through an interpreter.

He approached the witness stand cautiously, like a hunter approaching wild game. He seemed unwilling to look directly at any of the lawyers or the jury. Instead, he sat sideways in the witness stand as if he were having a conversation with the wall.

From the start, his answers were circular and vague. Even when it came to provable facts, Marín refused to respond to questions directly. When he was shown his letter of termination and asked why he no longer works at Evans Fruit, he said, "Honestly I just don't understand what the reason was."

To get at how sexual harassment was handled at Evans Fruit, the government lawyers asked Marín what was expected of him, as orchard foreman, if someone reported an incident of sexual harassment. He replied that he didn't think there was much he could do. He could call the police or move the worker to a different crew. He said there wasn't anything more he could do beyond that because he would never be able to prove anything. Investigating the complaints was "not my responsibility," he said.

When asked about a crew leader under his watch who had supposedly exposed himself to other workers in the orchard, he said, "I was in charge of the orchard but it wasn't my job to straighten up adults," he said. "They're not children."

Marín then went on to deny more than two dozen specific incidents of sexual harassment that had been lodged against him at the trial. In addition to disavowing the accusations, he said that he didn't know nearly a half-dozen women who had made claims against him.

When it was the company lawyers' turn to ask Marín questions, they focused on the many tasks Marín tackled in a day to show that there was no way he had time to harass women for several hours at a time, as the workers had alleged.

Later, back at his home in Sunnyside, Marín said that he had felt calm on the witness stand because he had nothing to hide. He said he thought the jury viewed him favorably and saw him as a "normal person." Then, echoing the lawyers for Evans Fruit, he added, that the women bringing the case and making accusations against him "make up stories to get money."

The jury began their deliberations on a Tuesday after eleven days of testimony. By the next afternoon, they had filed back into the courtroom with a verdict. A handful of anxious workers took up half of the rear rows of the courtroom wearing white paper butterflies on their lapels as a symbol of hope and justice. The seats in the front row, where Bill and Jeannette Evans had watched the entire trial, were conspicuously empty. The verdict would be read without them.

The jury foreman handed the verdict form to the law clerk, who handed it to the judge, who reviewed the page without expression. The judge handed the form back to the clerk and she read the document aloud. The clerk named each of the fourteen women who had testified in the case and stated that for each one, the jury had found that she had not been sexually harassed while working at Evans Fruit. It was a complete victory for the company.

The women and the government lawyers sat in a kind of stunned silence. The Evans Fruit attorneys were decorously stoic. The Evanses arrived at the courthouse after court was adjourned. They had rushed in from their office and learned the good news from a court security guard on their way in. They quickly huddled with their attorneys in the courtroom.

Out in the parking lot, the jury members got into their cars to drive home to Ellensburg or Kennewick. Before he drove off in an SUV, Bill Huntington, a juror from Walla Walla, said he didn't feel the women had proved their case. "We all felt pretty much that there was some level of harassment but they did not establish it beyond a reasonable doubt," said Huntington, who unwittingly cited the wrong legal standard for civil cases. "But the claimants could be more proactive or flat-off quit and say they're going to the owners. And these things came up two to three years later. It's not so much that we believed Juan Marín. But their stories lacked consistency. And they had problems in other areas. It's easy to believe they had gotten together and compared notes. But I felt the Evans[es] could have done better.

"I hope the Evans[es] will realize that they need to be more vigilant in their sexual harassment policies," Huntington said. "It seemed they were in denial. They trusted Juan Marín and they didn't think it could happen. They were a little too reliant on him."

By now, the Evanses had emerged from the courthouse. Standing next to his white Cadillac Escalade, Bill Evans said he felt "very happy." He said, "It is a great win. It all comes down to accountability and credibility."[13]

As for Juan Marín, "I am very disappointed in him," he said.

Before getting into the car, Bill Evans joined a conversation between his wife and the jury foreperson, Cameron Fisher, who used to work for the Washington State Department of Labor and Industries.

Fisher suggested that Evans Fruit should modernize its operations by hiring a professional human resources staffer. "You have to get on with the times and with the way things are run today," Fisher said.

Jeannette thanked the foreman for the tip before getting behind the wheel of the Escalade. The couple headed east on Yakima Avenue to the Dairy Queen where they celebrated with ice cream.

About a year after trial, the U.S. Equal Employment Opportunity Commission appealed the verdict in the Evans Fruit case. It argued that the company had inappropriately racialized the case to discredit the women who had testified about sexual harassment and assault. "The company's lawyers reinforced their racist theme that this was effectively a case brought by dishonest brown people against two innocent white people," the government's appeal brief said.

The commission argued that in opening arguments, an Evans Fruit attorney had unnecessarily introduced the issue of race when he told the jury that the U.S. Equal Employment Opportunity Commission "is trying to demonize Mr. and Mrs. Evans as the white people on the hill who don't care for the Mexicans. That's going to be their theme."

The company had also played "the poverty card" by disparaging their socioeconomic status at trial, the government said. The company denied that this was the case, but whether Evans Fruit's lawyers did or did not bring up race and class in a way that had been inappropriate was never decided on by the courts. In 2016, after nearly two more years of post-trial litigation, the case resulted in a draw when the company and the government agreed to settle the case once and for all. In doing so, neither the company nor Marín admitted any liability or wrongdoing.

The Evans Fruit case exposed an ugly, unspoken side of farm work but, by most accounts, the lawsuit has prompted change in the fields and orchards of Eastern Washington. At Evans Fruit specifically, the U.S. Equal Employment Opportunity Commission's involvement inspired the company to draft its first-ever sexual harassment policy in 2008, two years after the first farmworker reported problems to the government. The company also created a confidential phone hotline for workers and one of its bilingual staff members is made available to take complaints.

Throughout the Yakima Valley, the lawsuit has motivated growers to develop bilingual sexual-harassment policies that provide clear avenues for reporting and require timely and thorough investigations that guard against retaliation. There has also been new energy directed at training workers and supervisors about sexual harassment. Some farms now require all new hires to watch a short video on the topic before they're allowed to start work—an idea that was developed with the help of Brendan Monahan, one of the lawyers who represented Evans Fruit at trial, who no longer represents the company.

"I think that this case has fundamentally changed the industry. I really do," Monahan said shortly after the trial. "And I say that from the perspective of somebody who represents a number of large employers in the industry. We've done trainings all across the industry so that crew leads, orchard managers, foremen, know how to identify sexual harassment, know how to document, know how to report it."

Blanca Rodríguez, one of the attorneys with the Northwest Justice Project, which represented some of the women in the Evans Fruit case, said the lawsuit has also encouraged more workers to come forward to report sexual harassment. As a result, the Washington state attorney general and the state's Human Rights Commission have begun to take on farmworker sexual assault cases.

Danelia Barajas, a single mother of three, was one of the Evans Fruit farmworkers who had come forward to accuse Juan Marín of sexual harassment. At trial, she had testified that the orchard foreman had asked her to show him her breasts, and that he had grabbed one of her breasts in his truck. She said she had tried to fend Marín off, but she had remained on the job because she didn't know how else to support her kids.

On the day that the trial verdict was handed down, Barajas was one of the people packing the courtroom, hopeful that the jury would find in their favor. The jury's decision left her shocked. She simply could not find reason in it.

Thinking back on the trial a few weeks afterward, she still couldn't. "I could see how they would not believe one woman but fourteen women went to court and they don't believe a single one?"

Nevertheless, Barajas had come to realize that she was not alone and that there were people who were willing to listen to the way women were treated in the orchard. The revelation had made her determined and emphatic about making her experiences known. "We went and told the truth," Barajas said. "We took a risk and they did not believe us, and I do not regret that, because in other ranches they are paying more attention to the supervisors. It was a step that we took so that other women would also dare to speak up."

3

Behind Closed Doors and Without a Safety Net

Most afternoons, June Barrett leaves the Miami apartment that she shares with her twin sister to take a ten-minute cab ride to the wealthy suburb of Pinecrest, Florida. By about five in the afternoon, she arrives at the home of Raymond and Marjorie, a one-story structure as long as a football field decorated with mementos from the couple's world travels.

Raymond and Marjorie are in their nineties, and in this house, they have raised five children, celebrated anniversaries and birthdays, and grown old together. It is here, in their home, that June Barrett does her work.

A woman of boisterous good humor, Barrett is one in a rotation of six household workers who help Raymond and Marjorie with their most fundamental needs. Barrett typically begins her sixteen-hour overnight shift by preparing and serving the couple a three-course evening meal. By request, shrimp appetizers and salad are on heavy rotation.

After dinner, Barrett helps Marjorie through the standard bedtime rituals of brushing her teeth and changing her clothes. She also makes sure Raymond takes his medication and then helps him in the bathroom. Once the couple is asleep, Barrett cleans the kitchen, the dining room, and whatever else needs tidying. On some nights, she's able to take a power nap during her shift, though just as often, Barrett is tending to Marjorie throughout the night because the elderly woman, who suffers from dementia, can't manage to fall asleep.

By about five in the morning, Barrett is giving Marjorie a sponge bath, and an hour later, she helps Raymond take a shower. Then she makes breakfast and gets Raymond set up in his office so he can send some e-mails. By nine, she is headed home.

Barrett's job—domestic work—is the crucial but unseen labor done behind the closed doors of private homes. It is the intimate and invisible work that happens in someone else's bedroom, bathroom, and kitchen. As a profession, it takes on many forms, from tending to disabled or elderly clients to cooking and cleaning and watching an employer's kids. Some workers live in their clients' homes, and some, like Barrett, go home at the end of a set number of hours. But there are few fixed hours or norms in domestic work, and a caregiver can perform a multitude of tasks since the way that people run their households or realize their daily rituals is personal and particular. Its broad range of conditions collides with a lack of industry regulations, so the risk of exploitation is real in domestic work—especially because it has been purposely excluded from various federal labor laws meant to protect workers from abuse.

Barrett's current job has become one of the best she's ever had in her thirty-plus-year career. She says her employer, Judy Aberman, Raymond and Marjorie's daughter, treats her with respect and pays her fairly. Though there's little uniformity in the industry when it comes to wages, paid time off, and even the type of work that is required of domestic workers, Barrett says that Aberman pays her and her colleagues a good wage and has realistic expectations for what can be accomplished in a shift. Her boss also provides Barrett and her co-workers with paid sick days and a week of vacation each year, which employers are not required to do under federal law. Another perquisite of her job: Aberman hands out a holiday bonus at the end of the year. "They are critical to the quality of life of my parents' lives," Aberman says. "How could you not take care of the people who are taking care of your family?"

Not all employers operate with the same philosophy, and Barrett, who is originally from Jamaica, hasn't been spared the abuses that can come with her job. She took her first job as a domestic worker at sixteen in Kingston after falling into the line of work out of necessity.

Barrett and her twin sister had been orphaned when they were two, and the girls were split up between family members a few years later. Barrett was sent to live in the rural outskirts of Montego Bay with an aunt who she says grudgingly took her in and never let Barrett forget that she was not only a burden but also "too dark." When Barrett finished public school at fifteen, she says her aunt made it clear that she was no longer welcome in her home.

Gutsy and self-possessed, Barrett talked her way into a domestic-worker training school run by the Methodist church, where she learned to iron, clean, and cook. After four months, the church placed her in her first job with the family of a government official who lived in a large house in Kingston. Still a teenager, she found herself in charge of running a busy household, but the family she worked for didn't think Barrett moved fast enough. After what they deemed to be slow service during a social event, they told her to pack up her things.

Going back to her aunt's house in the countryside wasn't an option, so Barrett hustled to find another job as a live-in domestic worker. Things become more complicated when she found out that she'd gotten pregnant by a man she was dating. He denied that he was the child's father, so she had to fend for herself, but without a job, she was also homeless. The pregnancy made her too sick to work, so she spent her days resting at the house where her twin sister worked as a domestic worker. In the evening, she stayed with a friend. The rest of the time, she wandered the streets of Kingston.

After a few months, she found a temporary job as a live-in domestic worker but it was not the solution she had hoped for. When she was eight months pregnant, her employer made a violent sexual advance toward her. Barrett didn't say anything because she thought she would be blamed for it, though staying silent didn't help her either. She took out her outrage on the women in the family, and she was fired.

Barrett found herself homeless again and she had nowhere else to go but back to her family in the countryside. She knew her aunt most certainly wouldn't take her in, but it turned out that her older sister couldn't accommodate her either. The only option was to stay in a room in their small village with her ailing and bedridden grandmother.

A couple weeks after she arrived, with the help of a midwife, she delivered her baby in the room she shared with her grandmother. Two months later, the baby died of meningitis. Barrett was devastated. She tried to cope with her loss by immediately heading back to Kingston to lose herself in work.

The first job she found was with a couple who needed help around the house and childcare for their two-year-old boy. The husband of the household was a loan officer at a nearby bank, and his wife had a long commute to a job at a phone company.

Fairly quickly, Barrett began to feel uncomfortable around her male boss because he brought lovers home with him during his lunch hour. Before long, he graduated to fondling and touching Barrett whenever his wife wasn't around. Then, a few months into the job, he became more aggressive and raped Barrett while his toddler slept in another room.

It happened more than once. "When he came back and did not have a woman with him, I knew I would be sexually abused that day," Barrett says.

This was Barrett's most extreme experience with on-the-job

sexual violence, though it wasn't her last. The ordeal served to reinforce how difficult it could be to extricate herself from a bad
live-in job. *What am I going to do?* Barrett remembers thinking at
the time. *I'm not allowed to go back home. Am I going to be in the
streets, homeless?*

After six months, she took another job while trying to find other
types of work. She enrolled in night classes at the local high school
focused on teaching technical skills, which led to a series of office
jobs. She liked the work, but at her second job as an office admin-
istrator, a co-worker outed her as a lesbian and the word got out.
She started receiving threats outside of the office—one man told
her that he would rape her straight.

The homophobia in her country made her fearful enough to
spend her savings on plane tickets to South Africa for a gay rights
conference and to London, where she spent eight months living
with a group of friends from the Caribbean, which gave her time
to recover from the stress of life in Jamaica. She thinks back on her
travels as one of the best times of her life, but the United States
beckoned. Barrett was inspired by what she saw in the movies
and in the news. She loved what America represented—a land of
freedom and human rights—and she imagined feeling safe there.

Barrett bought a plane ticket to New York. She had a few extended relatives in the Northeast, including a cousin in Connecti-
cut who picked her up from LaGuardia Airport. To earn a living,
she went back to domestic work; she found a job in New Jersey
caring for the children of a divorced man. Barrett loved the work
and the family, but although she became a U.S. citizen in 2005, she
didn't have authorization to work in the United States at the time.
Her boss had no choice but to let her go.

He was aware that employing an undocumented worker was a
risky proposition. It is illegal to hire undocumented immigrants,
and though the government has historically focused on deporting

workers rather than punishing employers, the consequences for companies and bosses include financial penalties and in some cases, criminal prosecution.[1]

Meanwhile workers in any industry who don't have the proper papers to work in the United States—whether they are hired to harvest vegetables or vacuum office buildings—operate from a position of economic precariousness. "To get work undocumented, it was difficult," Barrett says.

The challenge of finding a job without valid work papers was what kept janitors like Georgina Hernández or farmworkers like Blanca Alfaro tethered to their jobs even if they were mistreated or abused. Barrett found a way out of her predicament when her sister, Judy, came to the rescue. Her twin was living and working in Florida as a domestic worker, and she helped Barrett find a temporary live-in gig in Miami. Barrett took a Greyhound bus from the Northeast to Florida. The job would give her room and board for a few months, but it didn't pay. While this type of arrangement is not uncommon in domestic work, it flouts minimum wage laws.

Nevertheless, the job bought Barrett some time to figure out her next move. It also forced her to confront a discordant reality: as a domestic worker in search of the American Dream, she had taken one in only a handful of jobs in the United States that has been excluded from laws meant to shield workers from abuse.

Laws that protect workers in the United States from exploitation date back to the federal programs launched in the 1930s under the New Deal. Among the key legislative reforms were the National Labor Relations Act of 1935, which gave workers the right to form unions and to bargain collectively for improved working conditions. Then came the Federal Labor Standards Act of 1938, which established requirements for minimum wage and overtime.

As these laws were being drafted, domestic workers and farmworkers were purposely excluded, a development that scholars attribute to the fact that they were jobs primarily done by African Americans.

As the country's most fundamental labor laws were crafted, white Southern legislators steeped in the legacy of slavery sought to maintain the racial hierarchies of the Jim Crow South and resisted extending worker protections to African American laborers. Knowing that Northern legislators would not approve—and federal law would prohibit—overt racial exclusions from these laws, excluding specific categories of work served as the next best option. "Since most southern blacks were employed as agricultural and domestic laborers, that occupational classification became an ostensibly race-neutral way to exclude blacks by proxy," Juan F. Perea, a law professor with Loyola University School of Law in Chicago, wrote in a paper about worker-related New Deal legislation.[2]

As labor done disproportionately by African American women, domestic work was further devalued and marginalized on the bases of both race and gender. Legal scholars Hina Shah and Marci Seville have argued that "the racial disdain for the black servant—'a despised race to a despised calling'—justified labeling the work as 'nigger's work.' As such, society easily disregarded domestic labor as not being real work, worthy of fair and equal treatment."[3] Premilla Nadasen, a historian and author of *Household Workers Unite: The Untold Story of African American Women Who Built a Movement*, similarly describes paid household work as a "degraded occupation" because it was work done in the domestic sphere by women of color.[4]

As federal protections for American workers have expanded, domestic workers have continued to be excluded. Today the vast majority of American workers receive paid family or medical leave, but these benefits are not extended to domestic workers. Caregivers, for the most part, still have no legal recourse from the federal government if they are discriminated against because of their age, disability, race, religion, or sex—which some enforcement agencies have recently interpreted to include gender identity and sexual orientation.[5]

There have been some improvements, however. Federal laws now include domestic workers when it comes to paying minimum wage and overtime, a reform that emerged out of overlooked but critical activism by African American domestic workers in the mid-1970s, the first movement to "put the issue of domestic workers' labor rights on the national political agenda," according to Nadasen.

Nadasen writes that this effort had some seemingly unlikely origins. It began with the National Committee on Household Employment, a group of liberal professional women who employed domestic workers. In 1969, the organization reoriented itself toward the interests of domestic workers themselves when black feminist Edith Barksdale-Sloan took on a leadership role. She and the National Committee on Household Employment brought local domestic worker groups together to create the Household Technicians of America.

To make the case that domestic workers should be included in federal minimum wage laws, the Household Technicians of America argued that they deserved fair treatment and pay because their work was like any other kind of honest day's work, an approach that garnered the support of labor union officials. Still, it took several legislative attempts before domestic worker organizers were able to overcome the opposition by congressmen who saw a bill regulating pay rates of household workers as an intrusion into personal domestic affairs. Nadasen writes that the male legislators were "fearful not only of 'irate' housewives but also a disruption of the gender division of labor and its consequences."[6] In other words, while legislators were dismissive of the domestic labor that their female partners did, they also simultaneously worried that increased wages would mean that it would be harder to find workers to do the cleaning and cooking that they personally didn't want to do.[7]

Nadasen notes that in the end, domestic workers took advantage of the inherent contradiction in the legislators' arguments. Their argument was compelling in its pragmatism: Failing to increase wages for household workers would create a shortage of them, and the liberated working women who employed them were unlikely to pick up the slack. That domestic labor, Nadasen writes, would likely fall on middle-class men like the legislators who had the power to decide the bill's fate.[8]

In 1974, after four years of trying, domestic workers were formally provided with federal minimum-wage benefits. More recently, in 2015, the U.S. Department of Labor extended federal minimum-wage and overtime protections to home-care workers.

Loopholes remain. Live-in domestic workers are not entitled to overtime, and those who provide companion care by providing nonmedical emotional and logistical help to disabled or elderly clients are exempted from both minimum-wage and overtime requirements.

The lack of regulations has not benefited the immigrant women who make up the majority of the industry's workforce today. Studies and surveys have found that domestic workers experience a range of job abuses related to pay, workload, and treatment.[9] There's no limit, for example, to what an employer can put on a domestic worker's to-do list, because the day-to-day of living is messy and variable. And because there isn't widespread agreement about how much a domestic worker ought to be paid, some employers exploit the lack of uniformity by illegally failing to provide the federal minimum wage.

Scholars Pierrette Hondagneu-Sotelo of the University of Southern California and Mary Romero of Arizona State University have each interviewed dozens of domestic workers in California and Colorado and found that domestic workers are subject to a wide range of treatment by their employers. For every thoughtful employer like June Barrett's boss, there are employers who are

exacting and punitive, and the intersection of the private sphere
and the workplace can be tense and confusing.

Myrla Baldonado, a former domestic worker who's now an organizer for the Pilipino Workers Center in Los Angeles, puts it this
way: "I've had nice experiences but it's hard to get because there
are no rules. There's no floor and no ceiling. You can do anything.
It's just luck."

With the majority of the country's more than 2 million domestic
workers migrating from regions such as Latin America, the Caribbean, and Asia, exploitative employers sometimes use workers'
tenuous immigration status to facilitate abuse. At its most extreme,
domestic workers are being trafficked to the United States and
coerced to work for physically and sexually abusive employers for
little or no pay.[10]

In a case that resulted in a federal criminal trial in 2010, a Texas
couple was found guilty of trafficking a domestic worker from Nige-
ria and then subjecting her to horrific abuses—including repeated
rapes by the husband—for about a decade. She had been unable
to escape because the couple had restricted her communications,
taken away her passport, and isolated her to such an extent that she
was almost unseen.[11]

At the end of the trial, the federal judge presiding over the case
didn't hide his shock at how the crime had been hidden for so
long behind closed doors. "It is frightening," the judge said. "This
woman was in the country for over ten years, and nobody was even
curious about her situation."[12]

Live-in domestic workers like the woman trafficked from Nige-
ria are the most susceptible to abuses. As documented in various
academic studies and industry reports, these workers report feeling that they are on the clock twenty-four hours a day because
they can't ignore the early-morning cries of a child or refuse to
assist an elderly client in the middle of the night.[13] Some have reported being forced to sleep in closets or on the floor in bedrooms

of children they were caring for. Caregivers also say they are not given time to eat or even personal access to the kitchen where they prepare their employers' meals.

In 2012 the National Domestic Workers Alliance conducted a first-of-its-kind survey of more than two thousand workers from all over the country and found grave abuses related to workload, hours, and pay. The resulting report, "Home Economics: The Invisible and Unregulated World of Domestic Work," also identified problems related to verbal, physical, and sexual abuse.[14]

"In some situations, abuse is laced with racial slurs or threats regarding immigration status," the report said. "In other instances, verbal abuse escalates into physical violence. And in far too many cases, it takes the form of sexual harassment and even sexual assault."

Echoing the concerns of night-shift janitors and farmworkers, few of these abused domestic workers complained, because they didn't want to lose their jobs, the survey found. Undocumented workers added that they worried that their immigration status would be used against them.

For domestic worker advocates, physical abuse like sexual harassment and assault has been difficult to bring up and address. "We're silent because of the mentality of servitude," says Allison Julien, a domestic worker organizer and a New York City nanny. "Your role is to be of service. Very few of us are taught to share our stories. That's why workers don't come forward even though we know there is sexual violence in the workplace."

Julien is a worker-leader who has organized domestic workers for more than a decade, and she says sexual abuse on the job is one of the hardest topics to broach. "We'll talk about overtime, but physical violence and sexual violence we find are hard topics to raise up because of the shame and judgment," she says. "There's such silence, and employers know that."

Sexual harassment is especially hard to pinpoint because

domestic work is intimate work done in someone else's home, where uncomfortable and offensive moments can be hard to parse and define. To deal with the situation, some workers actively normalize sexual harassment. "There is a numbing-out aspect to this in order to survive," Julien says. "So the thinking is, 'It's not that bad.' That's why they keep going back to work."

Domestic workers who experience sexual harassment also find themselves without a strong legal safety net. Title VII, the part of the Civil Rights Act of 1964 that makes workplace sexual harassment illegal, applies only to employers who have more than fifteen employees, rarities in domestic work.

Abused domestic workers can choose to file criminal charges, but the gap in workplace civil rights laws leaves most caregivers without clear legal recourse in civil courts. Some counties or states—but certainly not all—fill in this gap with local ordinances or laws.

Florida, which doesn't have a state department of labor, is one place where domestic workers have no direct way of bringing a workplace sexual harassment claim. So when a previous employer groped and grabbed June Barrett in his Miami home, the domestic worker wasn't wrong when she thought that she just had to put up with it.

Before Barrett landed her current job with Raymond and Marjorie, she passed through a number of households that showed her just how many ways she could be dehumanized at work. After the stopgap job in Miami that didn't pay, Barrett took a live-in job that involved taking care of a woman's aging parents.

The job was a lifesaver, but she was on call around the clock. She rarely had time for uninterrupted sleep, and when she was given a day off—which usually required a bit of cajoling and begging—she would check herself into a hotel so she could get some rest.

The elderly couple she cared for were verbally abusive. The

husband shouted at her to work faster. The wife made racist remarks like, "Make sure you don't touch me, you cotton-pickin' nigger."

But quitting suddenly wasn't a real option. "I had anxiety attacks because, where am I going to go?" she said. "I would be homeless in Miami. So you have to stick it out and you go to your room and cry."

In search of a way out, Barrett went to a placement agency, which are largely unregulated and have a reputation among workers for turning a blind eye to complaints and concerns. Nevertheless, they offer a convenient way for employers and workers to find each other, and Barrett was sick from stress and desperate to escape the couple she was working for.

It was a relief when the agency finally placed her in a new live-in job caring for an elderly man with vision problems. The workload was more reasonable, but in the end, the job was no improvement.

The warning signs came immediately, on her first night on the job. Barrett was helping her employer into bed when he ordered her to lie down with him. She declined and told him that he was being unprofessional. Unrepentant, he told Barrett that other caregivers had done it and she would be no different. Barrett walked out and went to her room, confused and unnerved.

The exchange turned out to be a prelude to a pattern of sexual harassment and assault. The next morning, as Barrett helped her new client in the bathroom, he grabbed her crotch. She protested and tried to shame him into stopping, but he didn't mind. Over the next few months, he took every opportunity to grab, grope, and kiss her.

Her employer's daughter witnessed the harassment but didn't take the problem seriously. Watching her father grab Barrett's breast, she treated it like a joke. "I couldn't believe it," Barrett says. "She was laughing. Because I was just a piece of meat, just the caregiver, I was nothing."

The job was stable and it paid well, but Barrett didn't know how long she could put up with her boss. She was confident that she could overpower his physical advances if necessary, but their interactions filled her with disgust. She called her sister Judy frequently for moral support, and they agreed that Barrett had to be practical about resolving the problem. For a time at least, she would just have to find a way to manage.

Barrett purposely didn't tell the agency what was happening because they were her lifeline to future work. "I didn't want them to think I was a whiner," she says.

Her strategy of saying nothing worked. By keeping her mouth shut about the sexual abuse for a few months, Barrett was able to secure fill-in domestic work through the agency, which was enough to keep her afloat until she found a job with regular hours.

As she searched for better work, Barrett found solace at the Miami Workers Center, an advocacy organization that promotes economic, gender, and racial equality. She had become a regular at workshops on topics such as women's empowerment, self-care, and dealing with racism. In 2012, she stepped up her commitment to the organization after the murder of seventeen-year-old Trayvon Martin in a neighborhood just a few hours from where she lived. The center had taken a vocal role in demanding justice for the teen, which the group ultimately saw as a matter of racial and economic justice. "I saw the power of organizing," Barrett says. "I was impressed."

Her work situation finally improved in December 2013, when her sister connected Barrett with her current job caring for Raymond and Marjorie. The family not only offered a job on fair terms; they also encouraged her activism.

The year before, the Miami Workers Center had become the permanent home for the Workplace Justice Project, a collaboration launched at the Florida Immigrant Advocacy Center with support from organizations like the Service Employees International Union (SEIU). They were pushing to improve the working conditions for domestic workers, and the project was receiving guidance from the National Domestic Workers Alliance. Barrett had jumped at the chance to get involved.

She began putting the paid vacation days she received from her job with Raymond and Marjorie toward events related to improving conditions for domestic workers. Her conviction inspired her boss, Judy Aberman, to support her activism with financial donations and by attending events where the employer gave impromptu speeches about the importance of treating workers fairly.

In the summer of 2016, the center hosted South Florida's inaugural Domestic Workers Assembly, which was attended by politicians, journalists, and two hundred domestic workers. The conference organizer, Marcia Olivo, says she wanted government officials and the public to become aware of the full range of problems domestic workers face so that they could begin to seek public policy responses.

"People don't see domestic work as real work and they don't recognize the things that happen in the industry," says Olivo, the center's executive director, "and part of what is going to help win more protections for them is to make people more respectful of the work."

Olivo asked Barrett to speak about sexual harassment in domestic work, but the caregiver was not initially inclined to do it. She gave it some thought and decided to set aside her trepidations after thinking of all of her friends in the industry who had been sexually harassed or worse—especially one friend who had felt pressured into sleeping with her boss. "I wanted to talk about it so that other people would talk about it," Barrett says.

On the day of the event, Barrett remembers walking to the microphone at the front of the room without notes because she intended to speak from the most honest place she could muster. She was nervous, but she began by expressing what she was feeling: "I'm so happy to be here," she said. "When women come together to organize for change, there is something very powerful about that."

The audience applauded, giving Barrett the confidence to continue. She launched into the story about the employer who had asked her to lie down with him and then embarked on a relentless campaign to touch her crotch and her breasts. She described how demeaning it had felt and said it shouldn't be tolerated as just part of the job. When she finished, the crowd applauded again, and Barrett says she could feel that the audience appreciated how much it had taken to share her story.

The feeling that came to Barrett in that moment surprised her. "I felt liberated," she says. "I had carried that shame that I had allowed this to happen. I felt I had allowed it to happen to earn money."

Saying it all aloud had excised that shame. "It's completely gone," she says.

By taking steps toward winning new protections for domestic workers at the local level, the Miami Workers Center is following a strategy that has been successful nationwide.

Changing the laws, state by state—sometimes starting with a single county or a city—has led to slow but steady gains for domestic workers. It's an approach promoted by the National Domestic Workers Alliance, which organizes nationally and acts as a strategic support group for the local organizations that are running the bills.

So far, eight states have adopted a so-called Domestic Workers' Bill of Rights, leading to improvements in pay and working conditions. Because the alliance believes that the legislation should be generated by the workers themselves and fought for from the ground up, each of these bills has been tailored to the specific needs and political climate of each state. Together, these grassroots legislative fixes have created a range of protections and benefits, such as mandates for overtime pay, rest breaks, written contracts, and paid time off, as well as safeguards from sexual harassment and labor trafficking.

This movement for law-based reform had its start in the late 1990s in New York City when Southeast Asian domestic workers banded together with Caribbean and Latina caregivers to start a worker-led advocacy group called Domestic Workers United.

Allison Julien, the nanny from New York City, has been on the front line of the organization's work since those early days. She had come to the United States in the 1990s from Barbados when she was in her late teens. When she started working as a caregiver in Manhattan, there was no overtime, no paid vacation and no enforceable law against sexual harassment for domestic workers.

She heard about Domestic Workers United in 2001, as the group started making noise about the industry's poor working conditions. The organization hosted rallies and public events where women talked about the incredible workloads they managed, how little they were paid, and sometimes the ways that their bosses had abused them. At first, Julien did not turn up for any of these events. "I never found out about these events until after they happened," she says.

Then one afternoon in the spring of 2002, she was at a park on the Upper West Side with the children that she babysat when an organizer from Domestic Workers United named Ai-jen Poo approached her. Poo would go on to become one of the founders of the National Domestic Workers Alliance, but that day, she was handing out flyers for Domestic Workers United's monthly meeting. Poo told Julien that the group was fighting for a proposed local ordinance that would make it easier for domestic workers to understand their rights on the job. She said that it was a step toward improving the work life of domestic workers, a way to begin growing employment rights by rewriting the law. For Julien, "it was a light bulb going on," and the nanny immediately joined the organization.

By then, Julien had experienced what many caregivers in the country know—that even good jobs with thoughtful families involve inevitable battles over things that most workers take for granted, such as vacation, sick time, and overtime.

One family in particular had made this clear to Julien. In 1997, she had been hired to care for the family's two young children, and after they were struck with the flu, Julien got sick, too. Feeling miserable, Julien took a couple of days off to recuperate. When she returned to work, her employer was upset and complained about what a problem it had been for the family that Julien had taken time off. "I remember saying to this employer, 'Next time I get sick, I'll ask God to make me sick on a Saturday or Sunday so as to not inconvenience you,'" Julien says.

"I saw the way that employers saw us," she says of that experience. "It is work that is overlooked and overshadowed and you are expected to perform without a complaint or without needing time to be with your family or see doctors."

In May 2003, nearly a year after Julien met Ai-jen Poo at the Upper West Side park, the New York City council voted in favor of the policy to improve domestic workers' awareness of their employment rights. With a victory and momentum, the group sought to improve conditions for domestic workers throughout the state.

An expanded group of organizations formed the New York Domestic Workers Justice Coalition to launch a campaign for a statewide bill that would provide the type of worker protections not offered to them through federal laws.[15] To set the priorities for the state bill, the group organized a convention in New York City. About three hundred domestic workers turned up to discuss the benefits that they wanted to fight for, such as paid time off, sick days, severance pay, health care, and protection from sexual harassment. The legislation, which the coalition called the New York Domestic Workers' Bill of Rights, was introduced in 2004.

To galvanize support, the group hosted marches and rallies where domestic workers described some of the working conditions they were forced to endure. At a 2004 event that was covered by the *New York Times*, a caregiver from Zambia named Estella Ng'ambi spoke about working eighteen hours a day, seven days a week, and getting paid $250 a month.[16] She wasn't given a bedroom and was forced to sleep on the floor behind the living room couch.

Ng'ambi's story wasn't unique. "There's a lot of abuse," Domestic Workers United organizer Erline Browne told the newspaper. "There's a lot of Estellas out there."

Even with the force of hundreds of workers lobbying for the New York Domestic Workers' Bill of Rights, combined with a growing public consciousness about the abuses domestic workers faced on the job, it took more than six years of political work before the bill passed in 2010. Julien, by then an activated organizer, was there at every step. Looking back, she says that the fundamental challenge that contributed to the long political battle had to do with the fact that policy makers did not initially see domestic work as real work. Lawmakers also had little incentive to push for domestic worker rights because some were undocumented and they were not viewed as a significant voting bloc.

So the coalition began to build alliances. It tapped sympathetic employers, as well as religious and student groups, to show support for the bill at hearings and events. "We brought in people who had the power to vote," Julien says. "It started to shift the legislators who didn't know where they stood on this."

Still, the bill hit repeated political headwinds, and the legislation had to be introduced three times. Throughout the process, the domestic worker coalition was relentless. Its members made regular lobbying visits to the state capitol, and as the years passed, the crowd grew stronger, from a couple dozen domestic workers arriving in cargo vans to hundreds of them turning up by the busload. "I can only think they were hoping we would go away but that was not going to happen," Julien says of the legislators. "We were called crazy a million times."

In 2010, the legislation cleared both houses of the state legislature and governor David Paterson said that he would sign the bill if it made it to his desk. When the bill was presented to him, he kept his word. "For me, personally, I exhaled," Julien says.

The efforts on the East Coast were infectious. As New York domestic workers fought for legislation, a grassroots organization of Latina immigrant women named Mujeres Unidas y Activas, and La Raza Centro Legal, a legal services organization dedicated to immigrant and low-income clients, were strategizing over the best way to support domestic workers in San Francisco.

They began with research. To learn more about what workers needed and wanted, the groups partnered with the San Francisco Public Health Department and a social-justice research organization called DataCenter, which trained immigrant women to conduct hour-long surveys of their peers—domestic workers they encountered in parks, on buses, and at laundromats. In 2007, the groups published a report, based on conversations with nearly 250 domestic workers, which found that many domestic workers don't get rest breaks or overtime and suffer emotional and physical abuse from their employers. The report concluded that domestic work "is a very vulnerable industry. Rampant abuses of household workers must be addressed."[17]

Even before the report was completed, worker advocates realized that the problems surfacing from the research were rooted in the fact that domestic workers are excluded from various federal and state labor laws. The California groups decided to pursue an approach similar to the one taken by New York domestic workers.[18] "It became clear that some kind of state policy to right historical wrongs was really important," says Andrea Cristina Mercado, who was then an organizer with Mujeres Unidas y Activas and later with the National Domestic Workers Alliance.

Similar conversations were happening in Southern California at community organizations that promote economic justice, like the Coalition for Humane Immigrant Rights of Los Angeles and

Filipino Advocates for Justice. In all, seven groups throughout the state joined together to advance an agenda to augment the rights of domestic workers. Like the conference in New York City that had jump-started the Domestic Workers' Bill of Rights, the California organizers began with a convening of domestic workers. At that meeting, the group came up with a list of more than a dozen priority items, ranging from overtime pay to family and medical leave, which became the blueprint for the legislation that the coalition would propose.

The reality of the legislative process hit the group fast. Most of these items, such as workers compensation or antidiscrimination measures, were not deemed politically viable by their legislative allies and were dropped by the time the California bill was introduced in 2006. The legislation instead focused exclusively on granting overtime and minimum wage to household workers.

Like their colleagues in New York, the California domestic workers faced a years-long political fight. Moreover, the California caregivers faced an unexpected adversary. Advocates of disability rights pushed back on the bill because they were worried that it would make in-home care unaffordable. To quell these concerns, the bill language was revised to clarify that the proposed law would not apply to casual babysitting or personal attendants working for the elderly or disabled.

With these changes, the bill cleared both houses of the state legislature, leaving the domestic worker advocates hopeful. The bill went to the governor for his signature, but a month later, Governor Arnold Schwarzenegger upset the worker advocates by vetoing it. In his veto message, it became clear that the domestic worker coalition had not yet done enough to address the concerns of the disability advocates. Schwarzenegger declined to sign the bill because it "subjects seniors and the severely disabled who hire household workers to a new cause for civil litigation," he wrote.

With new insights into the legislative process, the coalition decided to try again when Democrat Jerry Brown became California's governor in 2011. They reached out to disability rights advocates to find common ground. They continued to meet with legislators to explain why the bill was important. And they connected with labor organizations with similar political interests. "We learned that domestic workers can't do it by themselves," Mercado says.

In 2011, a bill dubbed the California Domestic Workers Bill of Rights was introduced. It called for overtime pay, rest breaks, paid vacation and sick leave, and protection from certain abuses. Once again, workers turned up in force to lobby for the bill at the state capitol. They worked with a lobbyist, and now they had the explicit support of legislators and labor unions.

The campaign also got a pop culture boost when Amy Poehler, the actress of *Saturday Night Live* and *Parks and Recreation* fame, agreed to do a public service announcement in favor of the legislation. Poehler had been vocal about her appreciation for the caregivers that make it possible to do her own job, and in a video distributed online, she asked viewers to support the bill for the same reason. "Many people ask me how I balance it all and the truth is it wouldn't be possible for me to do all those things without the help I get in my home every day," Poehler said in the video. "Every day, so many working women get to do what they do because there are wonderful people in their home, helping them. These workers, who inspire and influence our children, who take care of our loved ones and our homes, have been excluded from basic labor protections for generations."

With this momentum, the California Domestic Workers Bill of Rights passed both houses of the state legislature and was forwarded to the governor's desk, which was now occupied by Brown, a pro-labor democrat.

Just like his Republican predecessor, however, Brown vetoed the bill because of lingering questions about how the legislation would affect the disabled and elderly. "It was shocking," Mercado says, "because all the disability rights groups have removed their opposition."

The proponents of the bill refused to accept defeat. They decided to introduce the bill again in the following legislative session three months later. This time, they developed broader statewide support from areas beyond San Francisco and Los Angeles. They also continued to talk to legislators about the reasons the bill was necessary and rehired the lobbyist to refine their strategy. They were also more proactive and disciplined about explaining to the public why the legislation was needed. "We complemented the grassroots strategy with insider strategy," Mercado says.

In 2013, another bill—the third try at California legislation to better the working conditions of domestic workers—was proposed. Its scope had been narrowed; it called simply for overtime pay for domestic workers who worked more than nine hours a day or forty-five hours a week.

As it had the year before, the bill cleared both houses of the state legislature. Once again, it was sent to the governor for his support or veto. Now, nearly seven years after the first domestic worker bill had been put forward in California, the coalition had forced the political winds to shift. Opposition had fallen away and the public now largely favored improved conditions for domestic workers. The governor signed the bill into law.

There was only one hitch to their legislative victory. The bill would expire after three years unless the coalition brought another bill to make it permanent. An emboldened and wiser group of domestic-worker advocates began the political work almost immediately. In 2016, before the law would have sunset, the California Domestic Workers Bill of Rights was made permanent with wide-ranging support from politicians and the public.

The successes of the legislative efforts in New York and California—as hard-won as they were—have prompted others.

Domestic workers in Illinois are among the most recent caregivers to secure additional labor rights. In 2016, they won the passage of a bill that gives them paid time off and minimum wage. It also tackled sexual harassment directly by revising the Illinois Human Rights Act so that it expressly includes domestic workers, who had previously been singled out for exclusion.

And in 2017, Nevada legislators passed two bills supported by the SEIU, which provide a number of new benefits to domestic workers. Caregivers there now receive overtime pay, and there are caps on meal and lodging deductions. Employers are also required to give workers at least one full day off per week.

Systematically and purposely ignored by federal labor laws, domestic workers have had to fight for their rights one city, one county, and one state at a time. But momentum has built on momentum. "The domestic workers bill of rights campaigns has provided a way for us to fight for immigrant and non-immigrant workers—and to win," says Mercado, who is now the executive director of New Florida Majority, which seeks to build the political power of marginalized groups such as minorities, immigrants, and youth. "At the end of the day, this is not just about changing the law. We needed to make domestic work visible and respected."

Myrla Baldonado left domestic work and the city of Chicago before she could have benefited from the passage of the Illinois Domestic Workers' Bill of Rights, though in many ways, her work and activism helped pave the way for its passage.

Petite and pixielike, Baldonado emigrated from the Philippines in 2007 when she was in her fifties. She was a human rights activist in her home country, and she took on full-time domestic work in the United States after a friend in the Philippines died and left four children in need of financial support. After nearly a decade, she still sends them the bulk of her paycheck.

When she started working as a caregiver, Baldonado had no experience or context for the job. She joined the industry later in life and had a hard time accepting the indignities that were imposed on her. She was particularly troubled by the sexual harassment she encountered on the job, a workplace hazard she had not anticipated.

Of the thirty jobs she has had over the course of six years, she says she has experienced sexual harassment in nearly a half dozen of them. All of the incidents were mortifying and upsetting, but some were especially traumatizing. There was the husband of a client who made sexual innuendos and who came into her room at night to grope her in the dark. There was the eighty-year-old man she cared for who constantly talked about sex, grabbed at her, and invited her into his bed when he was naked. There was the son of a client who wanted to talk to her about dildos.

Out of embarrassment, Baldonado didn't do or say anything when these things had happened. Nowadays, she recognizes the irony: "I was a human rights activist in the Philippines, and I don't know why I was putting up with this," she says.

In 2011, domestic work and activism began to merge for Baldonado. Mechthild Hart, a co-founder of a workforce training and support organization called the Chicago Coalition of Household Workers, got in touch with her. Hart wanted to know if Baldonado would be willing to volunteer with Latino Union, a Chicago-based organization dedicated to improving the working conditions of immigrant workers and day laborers. The organization needed help recruiting Asian domestic workers for a survey that was being conducted by the National Domestic Workers Alliance. Baldonado agreed and took on the task with her usual aplomb. Hart could see that Baldonado had a knack for finding and reaching other domestic workers, and after she nominated Baldonado to speak about her experiences in domestic work at a town hall in Washington, D.C., the caregiver transitioned into a job as an organizer for Latino

Union. In her new role, the problem of sexual harassment in the industry continued to trouble her.

She has a distinct memory of a Latina domestic worker who came to her and said that she had been forced to have sex with the husband of a client. The worker wanted to make a report to the police, but she was undocumented and felt stuck in her job. She was one of the few who had come to discuss on-the-job sexual violence directly with Baldonado, even though the organizer knew that there were others.

The depth of the silence was obvious to Baldonado; in a support group that she helped run for victims of violence, women always showed up, but very few wanted to speak. "Sometimes they would sit and just cry and say, 'Next time I'll be able to talk,'" Baldonado says. "It's so shameful. The shame is there. You see so many immigrants who are so ashamed to tell their stories."

In 2015, Baldonado moved to Los Angeles to work for the Pilipino Workers Center, one of the organizations that helped pass the California Domestic Workers Bill of Rights. She has found that even with a change in job, demographics, and location, the workers she organizes remain uneasy about discussing sexual harassment on the job.

"It's the shame," she concludes.

Baldonado knows firsthand how social, cultural, and religious expectations can make it hard to talk about the problem, and she has felt how damaging it is to be judged for it. In 2012, Latino Union hosted an event to honor a Chicago exhibit recognizing domestic workers on International Human Rights Day, and Baldonado had been tapped to introduce Ai-jen Poo, the Domestic Workers United organizer who was now the executive director of the National Domestic Workers Alliance. During her remarks, Baldonado shared her experiences of sexual harassment and assault as a domestic worker.

Afterward, one of Baldonado's friends, another Filipina, privately chastised her for failing to be more modest in public. "Why would you say that?" her friend had demanded. Baldonado still remembers her response with clarity: "I said: Who will say it if I don't?"

The domestic worker–turned–organizer says she has been made bold by her experiences in the Philippines, where she had been an antidictatorship activist. In 1983, she was arrested and tried after the government accused her of being a subversive. She remembers what it was like to be scrutinized in court, how indignant she felt about being on display and having her experiences questioned and doubted. Her trial dragged on for two years, and she remained in detention the entire time. "There was a suspension of rights," says Baldonado. "They also made up charges like weapons possession so I couldn't get bail."

As a political detainee, she was moved from detention centers to "safe houses" so that no one, not even her family, knew where she was. She was chained to the bedpost of a guard's bed and forced to sleep on a blanket on the floor. Her captors tried to make her divulge the identities of other activists through weeks of water torture. She is proud that she never gave up a single name.

After two years, a judge found in her favor and he released her in 1985.

Baldonado says her courtroom experience in the Philippines is what made it possible for her to speak about sexual violence in the United States: She had already overcome the devastating experience of being publicly judged.

Even so, it remains difficult for Baldonado to confront the issue. In 2016, a few months before the Illinois Domestic Workers' Bill of Rights became law, she went back to Chicago for an event sponsored by Healing to Action, an organization that works to combat workplace sexual violence.

The audience heard from a panel of women who had been sexually harassed and assaulted while working in a hotel, a casino, a restaurant, and a factory. Baldonado was the lunchtime keynote speaker. For weeks, she had fretted about what to say. She felt especially anxious because she knew there would be other Filipinas in the audience, including her sister, whom she had never talked to about the sexual harassment and assault she had experienced. Baldonado worried that by speaking about sexual violence, she would bring shame to her community and her family and that it would turn them away from the issue altogether.

Baldonado decided to make her uncertainty part of the speech. "Of all of the abuses in the domestic worker workplace, sexual violence is the one that is less talked about," she said. "Why so? Because there is shame, fear of losing a job, retaliation, fear of deportation, language barriers, and ignorance of workplace laws that make us silent."

She said that she was going to tell the audience about the sexual harassment that she experienced as a caregiver. But first, she offered a preface. "Honestly, before I decided to give more details of the sexual harassment I encountered, I consulted my friend and mentor Mechthild Hart about the possible embarrassment that you and I might get from this experience," she said. "And she said, 'Okay, just get over it!'"

The crowd erupted in laughter but became quiet again as Baldonado continued recounting the advice she had received from Hart, who had added, "If we don't get over it, then it means you are still accepting the blame for what happened to you."

With that, Baldonado began to share examples of the sexual harassment she had experienced as a domestic worker. She closed by telling the audience that she was speaking that day to counter the stigma and shame that society puts on sexual violence victims like herself.

She was there that day, she said, with the intention of being vocal and defiant.

4

When Only the Police and the Prosecutor Believe You

To Guadalupe Chávez, the roads that snaked around the endless acres of farmland in California's Lost Hills had begun to take on a cruel similarity. Almond orchards gave way to yet more almond orchards, which bled into unending stands of pistachio trees, their branches a blur of leafy green as she drove.

A recently widowed mother of two from Mexico with no immigration papers and little English, Chávez supported her family with farm work. But she didn't know these orchards. In the red pickup truck ahead of her was the man who stood between her and an overdue paycheck. He was a supervisor with a local farm labor contractor. When they'd met near the farm, he'd told her the missing check was with his brother, and they needed to find him. Follow me, he'd said.

She thought of her unpaid bills and her two young sons. She started the car. He led her down one road, then another. They started and stopped, first at an aqueduct, then at a couple places near the side of the road, and then a shed. As they drove, they talked on the phone, and he asked her questions about where she lived, whether she liked to go dancing.

After she arrived at each location, he would tell her that they still weren't in the right place and they needed to keep driving.

Chávez found the whole thing strange, but she thought that they were looking for the man with her check. So she continued in a mix of apprehension and determination. She needed that check.

Suddenly the supervisor drove straight into the orchards themselves. She followed into a muddy grove, now blinded by the symmetry of the trees. This is when she began to feel scared. The supervisor got out of his truck and walked to her driver's side window. There's nobody here, he told her. Chávez asked about her check.

I have your check, he said. If you give me your underwear.[1]

What? Chávez said.

If you give me your underwear, he replied. Or do you want me to take them off of you?

She protested but he insisted: Do it fast or I'm gonna do it for you.

He added, You could scream, but it wouldn't make a difference because nobody can hear you way out here.

Chávez couldn't think straight. *Did he have a gun? Would he get violent?* She didn't know the way out.

She hiked up the ankle-length skirt she was wearing, pulled off the shorts she had on underneath, and took off her underwear. He told her to open up her legs. Then, Chávez says, the man raped her with his fingers.

Afterward, panicked, she asked him where they were so that she could leave and go home.

He told her to follow him out of the orchard. Before they drove off, he handed her the $250 paycheck she had earned for a week of picking pomegranates. He got in the truck and drove ahead. But before they were out of the trees, he stopped and approached Chávez's car again, this time with his pants undone. "Do you like to suck it?" he asked her.

She didn't know what he would do if she refused, so she said yes. He ejaculated on her sweatshirt and the side of her face. When he was done, he pointed straight ahead. The main road was there, not far. He told her not to say anything about what had happened. And he handed her underwear back to her.

Crying, she cleaned herself up with a tissue and then drove home too fast. She tried to remind herself that there was nothing else she could have done. She didn't know these roads. She had been afraid that he might kill her. She had thought it would just be easier to say yes to whatever he was asking.

She still blamed herself for the whole thing. As she drove, she wondered if God would forgive her. She searched for the logic in what happened. "It was my check," she says. "It was my money. I worked for it. Why did I have to do that to get my check? Why did I have to do that?"

Chávez eventually did something that rarely happens among people who say they've been sexually assaulted. She talked to the police. The vast majority of sexual assaults and rapes—about two-thirds, according to the federal government—are never reported to law enforcement. It's not hard to understand why.

Many women blame themselves for what happened because they think that they could have done something to stop it.[2] It's a rationale that doesn't apply to other violent crimes, such as armed robberies or attempted murders. Nevertheless, self-blame is one of the most cited reasons that women don't report sexual violence, along with embarrassment, fear of not being believed, and a distrust of the criminal justice system.[3]

Beyond the basic impulses to keep things a secret out of shame and fear, victims may be afraid or skeptical of the criminal justice system. "Victims of sexual violence can have a rough time in the criminal justice system and it scares them off," says David Lisak, a clinical psychologist who studies the causes and consequences of violence. "They have heard and seen victims who do come forward, who become the targets, basically, of pretty intense negative mischaracterizations."

There's evidence to ground these concerns. A 2016 U.S. Department of Justice investigation into the operations of the Baltimore Police Department found it to be dismissive of sexual assault victims. According to the report, "Detectives fail to develop and resolve preliminary investigations; fail to identify and collect evidence to corroborate victims' accounts; inadequately document their investigative steps; fail to collect and assess data, and report and classify reports of sexual assault; and lack supervisory review."[4]

Even police departments that aggressively investigate sexual assault cases and treat victims with sensitivity face a universal challenge: A delay in reporting makes it harder to collect evidence. For some victims, it can take weeks or even years to feel ready to report a sexual assault to the police.

Alice Vachss, a former New York City prosecutor who has personally tried more than a hundred sexual assault cases and supervised hundreds more, recalls one case in which the defense attorney asked a sexual assault victim why she had taken so long to report the crime. "And she said, 'I wasn't sure I wanted to be here,'" Vachss recalls, "and the defense attorney said, 'What do you mean?' And she said, 'I wasn't sure I wanted to be sitting in this chair answering your questions.'

"This is how people feel about it—that it's painful," says Vachss, author of *Sex Crimes: Then and Now*. "The amazing thing to me is that so many victims are willing to prosecute for nothing more than that little piece of justice that they might get at the end."

Immigrants in particular, face formidable barriers to reporting the crimes to law enforcement.[5] A 2007 study found that they are less likely to report crimes or contact the police for help compared to native-born Americans.[6] Studies have found that the fear of deportation influences Latinas in particular in their willingness to seek police assistance.[7] A federally funded study published in 2010 that examined the tendency of Latinas to report sexual assault to the police found that only one in fifteen sexually assaulted Latinas did so—fewer than the general population as a whole.[8] The less familiar the women in the study were with American laws and culture, the less likely they were to come forward. Some of the reasons they cited for not asking the police for help were related directly to their immigration status, including language barriers and fear of deportation.[9]

Sexual assault at work is shielded by yet another barrier to reporting the crime: fear of losing the job.[10] When work opportunities are scarce and financial pressures are unyielding, the calculation becomes unfathomable.

In 2005, Erika Morales was faced with this very quandary. She cleaned banks on the night shift as a janitor in California's Central Valley for ABM Industries (formerly American Building Maintenance), one of the largest such companies in the country. The only person she came into regular contact with was her supervisor, José Vásquez, a broad-shouldered man with salt-and-pepper hair. Unbeknownst to her and ABM, Vásquez was a convicted sex offender, and the company had already received complaints that the supervisor had sexually harassed women workers.

Vásquez began to give Morales a strange feeling when he started to appear, like a ghost, at her worksite to watch her as she vacuumed or scrubbed bathrooms. In addition to staring at her and making sexual comments, she says the supervisor sneaked up behind her and grabbed and groped her.[11]

She was disgusted and ashamed of the abuse, but she stayed on the job for a while longer. She wanted to quit, but as a single mother with two children, she couldn't figure out how she'd be able to go without a paycheck until she found a new job. "In that moment, I was going through a situation where I couldn't stop working," she says. "In that moment, the father of my children wasn't there. I was alone with the kids and I didn't have any other source of income for myself or my two kids. So I had to hope that it would change."

She figured it would take weeks of filling out applications before she could land a new job and didn't know how she would feed her children in the meantime. "That was one of the important reasons why I didn't leave the job," she says.

She tried to appeal directly to Vásquez instead. "I would say, 'Please don't keep doing this to me. I need the job. I truly need it. I need my kids to eat. I need to pay my rent, pay my bills. Please, I don't want to go through this,'" Morales says.

Vásquez only laughed. "People always say, 'Say no and they will stop,'" Morales says. "I would say it and he still wouldn't stop."

The janitor finally turned in her keys and quit after she says Vásquez attacked her in a supply closet one fall evening. "That's when I said, 'No more. I can't stand this,'" she says.

Morales is now a popular Spanish-language media personality in California's Central Valley, and she has counseled her audience not to stand for sexual harassment at work. "It's *your* work and it's not fair," Morales says. "It's not fair for women or for anyone that this happens to, that someone could take advantage of their power in whatever job they're in. I'm not only talking about janitors either. No, this happens everywhere."

Guadalupe Chávez says she also had the weight of providing for two children on her mind when the supervisor made his demands in the orchard. "When he wanted all of that, I felt more obligated," Chávez says. "And I always thought about my children."

Not every victim will choose to report the crime or move forward with pressing charges, nor should they feel pressured to do so. But the dynamics of immigrant labor, which leave workers exploited but unprotected, mean that an unscrupulous supervisor with a paycheck can extract just about anything from his workers.

Guadalupe Chávez grew up in Guadalajara, Mexico. She began working at her father's fruit stand when she was about eight, as soon as she was old enough to count change. By her teens, she had set up her own stall selling limes and oranges. The memory of the lively bustle of the streets of her hometown still makes her nostalgic.

Her family made the move to the United States in 1989 when their fruit business faltered. Chávez came to the country with her parents and four siblings, landing in rural California where most of her mother's family had settled. Chávez remembers finding it so quiet and dull compared to her life in the city. She hoped that she would be able to go to high school, but her parents told her that they needed financial help. She took a job as a babysitter before finding more reliable work at the many farms in the area. Agricultural work suited Chávez, who discovered that she loved the open air and the physicality of working in the fields.

When she was twenty-two, she got married to a man named Juan whom she had met in a night-school English class. They had two kids in three years. He was an attentive and present father who helped change diapers and bathe the kids. She loved that he had an innate sense of justice, she says.

Juan's stable job in an orange orchard allowed Chávez to spend her days taking care of their two boys and taking adult education classes. Juan noticed how much work Chávez did, between raising the kids and running the household, so on the weekends he took the whole family out for dinner so she didn't have to cook. "I don't think I'm going to find another man like that," Chávez says.

That life was upended on Christmas Day of 2005. Chávez was at home with the boys while her husband visited his family on his way home from work. But he never came home. The next morning, the phone rang and she remembers the voice on the other end of the line saying that Juan had been in a car accident and that he had died. Chávez could hear the words but she couldn't immediately process them. The depth of the tragedy became real to her only when she went to pick up Juan's truck and saw all of the Christmas gifts, now stained with blood, that he had been bringing home in the back seat.

There was nothing to do but mourn and start again.

Chávez had been living in housing provided by the orchard where Juan worked, and when he died, Chávez and her two sons were asked to move out. That's also when she discovered that her husband, an American citizen, hadn't started the citizenship process for her, so she was still in the country without documentation.

She found herself back in the precarious place of looking for work without immigration papers. She turned to jobs that she knew she could get. In nearby Hanford, she found work in a restaurant. Then she and her sons headed to the neighboring city of Corcoran, where Chávez went back to working in the fields.

Like many farmworkers in California, Chávez found jobs through a third-party farm labor contractor. Eventually, in the fall of 2006, she got a job picking pomegranates. She had been on the job for only about a week when she had to go looking for that missing paycheck—and then ended up having to sacrifice too much to get it.

Chávez says she hadn't planned on going to the police to report the assaults in the orchard. She had driven straight home, and because she didn't want her kids to see how upset she was, she went to her bedroom, crawled into bed, and cried herself to sleep. She woke up when the supervisor called her again and asked to come over. She was shocked, disgusted. She told him no.

Chávez didn't want to go back to work, but she needed the money. She knew there was another paycheck due to her soon that could float her for a while longer, but to get it, she'd have to see that supervisor again.

Feeling stuck, she called the only person she could think of who could help. Alegría de la Cruz was a lawyer with California Rural Legal Assistance in Fresno. Chávez had gone to see de la Cruz a few months before to report that she had been sexually harassed by another supervisor while working for another farm labor contractor, and the legal organization had suggested that she think about reporting the problem to the state's Department of Fair Employment and Housing.

Chávez told the lawyer that now she needed help getting an overdue paycheck. De la Cruz detected a familiar tension in Chávez's voice, and the lawyer asked the farmworker to come into the office. Later that day, Chávez turned up at the nonprofit's downtown Fresno office. The farmworker repeated that she needed a missing paycheck, but then, as if confessing a sin, Chávez admitted that she was having some pain in her uterus. "It was immediately clear that something else was going on," de la Cruz says.

De la Cruz and a community worker named Irma Luna took Chávez to a conference room. After a bit of prodding, the whole story tumbled out: The paycheck, the orchard, the wild goose chase, the assault. This was de la Cruz's first case of a reported workplace sexual assault, but over the years, she says, she has come to recognize a pattern to the exploitation, and Chávez fit the profile. Single women are especially vulnerable to sexual harassment in the fields, and women who are sexually harassed once are targeted for yet more harassment. As another client once told De la Cruz, "It's like they're sharks and we are injured and trailing blood in the water."

Chávez eventually agreed to go to the hospital to get her pain checked out. During the intake, a medical assistant named Fabby Martínez asked Chávez some routine health questions and wanted to know the last time Chávez had had sex.

Chávez's head fell. She told Martínez that she hadn't really had sex and then explained what had happened to her. Martínez responded by telling Chávez, "Honey, you shouldn't stay quiet."

Martínez asked the farmworker if she could call law enforcement, and Chávez nodded. The Kings County Sheriff's Department sent a senior deputy sheriff named Kristopher Zúñiga to interview Chávez at the hospital. As they spoke, he looked for holes in her story and facts that he could readily confirm. He ended the interview inclined to believe that Chávez was telling him the truth. He went into investigation mode.

The farmworker mentioned that she still had the unwashed clothes that she had been wearing on the day of the rape, so after the interview, he went to Chávez's house to pick them up as evidence. Chávez also gave him the supervisor's business card.

Next, one of Zúñiga's coworkers went looking for Chávez's supervisor. The next day, Zúñiga interviewed the suspect for about forty-five minutes. A Spanish-speaking sergeant helped Zúñiga translate his questions into Spanish and the suspect's answers into English.

It was the kind of halting, circuitous conversation that made Zúñiga suspicious. At first, the supervisor claimed that nothing had happened—he insisted that he had handed Chávez her paycheck at the shop, end of story. When Zúñiga kept pushing him, the suspect acknowledged that he and Chávez had driven together toward the Lost Hills.

Under more questioning, the supervisor finally told Zúñiga that after he had given Chávez her check near the fields, she had asked him for directions to the Lost Hills. He offered to show her the way. At some point, they stopped in the orchard, and they were about to go their separate ways when Chávez came on to him. He said that Chávez was the one who had volunteered to give him her underwear. She had also been the one who wanted to masturbate him with her hand, and it was Chávez who had asked him to ejaculate on her. Chávez had asked him to penetrate her with his fingers, he said.

During the interview, Zúñiga traded thoughts with his partner in English, at one point telling his partner that he simply did not believe the suspect's story. "He's not telling me the truth," Zúñiga said. "My guess is this is not the first time he's done this either. . . . Because these girls want their check. They want the money because they need their money so he has a hammer on 'em because he's got the check, and what do they do? . . . They're probably not gonna report it. Why? Because then they're gonna get fired and they need their jobs."

In an attempt to provoke a candid response, Zúñiga told his partner to ask the suspect: Why would Chávez ask a stranger to do these things to her? And why would she bother to report all of this to law enforcement if it had been consensual? "She has nothing to gain," Zúñiga said.

Zúñiga closed the interview by telling the suspect that he had basically helped corroborate Chávez's story, even down to what she was wearing. Just before turning off the tape recorder, Zúñiga told his partner that he believed Chávez: "Yeah, she's believable; he's not."

The victim of a sexual assault is expected to prove the veracity of her claims in a way that doesn't happen with any other crime. Her clothing, her behavior, and her decisions are considered fair game for scrutiny. As the thinking goes, even if she didn't want it, she may have asked for it.

Skepticism of sexual assault victims is neither a modern development nor an accident. Though these cases are described as he-said, she-said cases, the woman's account is seldom given equal consideration, and the tradition of discounting what she said is deeply embedded in the wording of our laws and reflects who, historically, has written them.

In her book *Redefining Rape: Sexual Violence in the Era of Suffrage and Segregation*, Stanford University history professor Estelle Freedman tracks how sexual assault laws have shifted over time to reflect changes in the role of women and people of color in society and political life. She notes that the definitions of sexual assault and rape have always been in flux, and over the centuries, the laws aimed at addressing these crimes have reflected who has been viewed as a citizen with the rights to bring a rape claim.

This has ultimately resulted in conditions favorable to white men, particularly in the nineteenth and early twentieth centuries. As Freedman notes in her book, during this era when women's suffrage had not yet been won and black segregation remained pronounced, it was white men who were writing and interpreting the rape laws in American statehouses and courtrooms, while women and minorities were explicitly excluded from political participation.

It is from this era that the stereotype of "real rape" emerges: that the victim is a woman of chaste character who valiantly tries to fight off an assault by a stranger.[12] Based on gendered and racialized notions of sexual assault, married women could not be raped by their husbands, the laws were disproportionately applied to criminalize African American men, and poor women or women of color could never be raped because they were never assumed to be of chaste character. "In the 19th and early 20th centuries, rape laws functioned to sustain white supremacy and to maintain male control and male sexual privilege," Freedman says.

The women's suffrage movement and the work of African American journalists like Ida B. Wells during this time period led to expanded rights for women and people of color, which created an avenue to recalibrate rape laws toward increasingly more equitable and realistic interpretations.[13] Nevertheless, rape myths became embedded in the legal system in a way that has been hard to shake.

Until the middle of the twentieth century, rape victims in many states were required to provide corroboration in court, such as physical evidence or eyewitness testimony, because their word alone was not considered enough.[14] Laws also required that a woman who had been sexually assaulted prove that she was of chaste character—often meaning she was a virgin—before she could be considered a rape victim.[15]

Nonwhite and poor women could never meet the requirements of chastity in the eyes of judges and juries on the very basis of their race and class. "You could never be raped if you had a sullied reputation or if you had sex before marriage, or if you were poor or a black woman because then you do not have standing of chastity to bring those claims," Freedman says.

These requirements have largely been excised from American law books. By the late 1970s, the requirement that rape victims provide corroborating evidence had largely fallen away.[16] And in an effort to guard against the chastity requirement, rape shield laws have also been passed in every state.[17] They include laws that make a victim's prior sexual history or other personal details off-limits in court.

But the legacies of corroboration and chastity die hard. Even though these requirements are no longer codified, in practice, corroboration and chastity often remain unspoken expectations. "Those things go very long and deep in our history," Freedman says.

These expectations can tip the scales against sexual assault victims. These are crimes largely committed in private. Eyewitnesses are unlikely. However, the notion that these are he-said, she-said crimes that are impossible to untangle and adjudicate is also a fallacy. Law enforcement—and workplace investigators examining cases of sexual harassment on the job—do, in fact, have other ways of delving more deeply into these types of claims.

David Lisak, the clinical psychologist, is a consultant to universities and the military on sexual assault prevention and policies. He says investigators can look for various types of information that would help them get to bottom of these scenarios. "The thing that I find frustrating about the he-said she-said thing is that most of the time, it's really a statement that covers over an inadequate investigation," Lisak says. "There is no doubt that there are some cases where there really are no other witnesses and there is no other evidence that can be mustered and you really are stuck. But in most cases, there is more evidence that can be brought to bear."

Lisak argues that a crime as serious as sexual assault will have some kind of impact on a victim, and skilled investigators can look for these types of changes. "If someone was assaulted and traumatized, it changes their social behavior, so you have a social network you can interview," he says. "It is still the case that too often, investigators aren't going far enough or deep enough."

Instead, there is a tendency to give perpetrators the benefit of the doubt as a way to guard against false reports. And it is undeniable that made-up claims of rape and sexual assault do, on occasion, occur.

Infamously, in 2006, Crystal Mangum was accused of lying about being gang-raped by members of the Duke University lacrosse team. The case was zealously prosecuted—but then it unraveled. The district attorney who pursued the case withheld evidence and was disbarred. Mangum's credibility was shot. Though Mangum maintains the rape happened, it was a troubling example of the ways in which the criminal justice system is ill-equipped to handle these cases.[18]

It's now held up as a cautionary tale, but it is also the exception that has helped reinforce a powerful misconception—that those who cry rape are often lying about it.

False reports *do* happen, but research shows that they are rare. Studies carried out in various countries have estimated that between 2 and 10 percent of claims appear to be untruthful.[19] To arrive at these numbers, researchers reviewed police reports and examined how the cases were classified by law enforcement, ranging from credible to false. Some studies also compared the police classifications with supplemental information from forensic examiners and victim service providers.[20]

One overarching methodological weakness of these studies is that law enforcement officials do not use a consistent definition of what should be considered a false report, or an unfounded case, in police parlance. Unfounded cases are those that, following investigation, lead police to believe that a report of rape or sexual assault is false or baseless. But sometimes, whether out of ignorance, a desire to close a difficult case, the inability to corroborate the assault, or a lack of cooperation from the victim, a report is erroneously deemed false by police.[21]

One of the most rigorous studies to examine false rape reporting to American law enforcement sought to counter this methodological problem. It was conducted by End Violence Against Women International, an organization started by a retired California police sergeant that provides training and resources to improve the investigation and prosecution of sexual assault. Researchers for this 2009 Department of Justice–funded study worked with eight police departments throughout the country, first to train the officers on the legal definition of "false report."[22] Next, researchers examined all of the sexual assault cases reported to these police departments for nearly two years. More than two thousand cases were included in End Violence Against Women International's "Making a Difference Project" study, and researchers concluded that 7 percent were false reports.[23]

The researchers eventually published their findings in *The Voice*, the magazine that is distributed by the National District Attorneys Association. They wrote that "the American public dramatically overestimates the percentage of sexual assault reports that are false."[24]

This overinflation is, in part, a product of the "stereotype of 'real rape,'" the researchers said. That stereotype often leads people to expect the perpetrator to be a "sick, crazy or deranged" stranger who brandishes a weapon before violently attacking the victim.[25] The stereotype also extends to the rape victim, who is expected to have few personal flaws—a modern-day iteration of the chaste character requirement—and to report the crime soon after the attack.[26]

The reality is that sexual assault cases are messy and difficult, and they can involve complicated people in compromising situations. In fact, the researchers from End Violence Against Women International argue that the myth of what constitutes a "real rape" has become so entrenched in the popular imagination that it affects the investigation, prosecution, and trial outcomes for victims.

In courtrooms throughout the country, prosecutors say that the rape myth and the fallacy that victims are lying about sexual assault is pervasive. "There is a mythology in pop culture that a rape victim is going to present to the ER battered with a black eye and with terrible bruising around thighs but the evidence is rarely that clear," says Joshua Marquis, a spokesperson for the National District Attorneys Association and a practicing prosecutor in Oregon.

He adds that he has found that juries tend to believe that false rape reports are frequent, when the reality is that it would be illogical for victims to lie because the criminal justice process itself can be so intense. "There are many, many opportunities for a victim to bail," he says. "They have to be very committed."

The believability of a sexual assault victim is further complicated by the fact that trauma can have the perverse effect of making a victim appear unreliable. A growing body of research into the neurobiology of trauma has found that the brain, after being exposed to a jarring event, does not respond the way we expect it to.

David Lisak travels across the country about a hundred days a year to teach law enforcement, military, and judicial personnel about how trauma affects the brain. His message is simple: The way the legal system works is out of sync with the latest brain science. "There's a huge lag between what we know from the research in neuroscience and what is getting implemented," he says.

In hotel conference rooms and police training halls, he uses a no-frills PowerPoint presentation to explain that during a life-threatening event, two chemicals—dopamine and norepinephrine—flood the brain. This jams up and alters the flow of information, which ultimately affects how victims process what is happening. "What people notice when they go through an experience like that is they say they can't think straight," he explains.

Simultaneously these chemicals modify the way the brain

encodes experiences, often making it difficult to remember things chronologically. "It results in flashes of memory, intense fragments," he says. "Fragments can, in many survivors, be really disconnected. What they remember are these vivid flashes of what happened, but they may have a lot of trouble answering questions about where or when was that, what sequence did it happen in, did this happen first or that?"

A victim who is having difficulty processing questions about a traumatic incident may appear suspicious. Taken out of context, the fitful memories of traumatized people can be devastating for their legal cases.

But even if the cops believe a victim, as they did in Guadalupe Chávez's case, it still might not be enough.

By the time Chávez's case came to Kathy Ciuffini, she had been a prosecutor for about half a decade. A deputy district attorney in California's Central Valley, Ciuffini had earned a reputation for taking on cases that other attorneys tended to avoid. She prosecuted a police officer who admitted to molesting teens and a gang leader who ordered a hit on a prison inmate.

Before that, she had been on the other side as a public defender, before realizing it wasn't the best fit. It was a job that put her on the fault lines of the justice system. On the one hand, she had defended a drunk driver at trial who she felt had been clearly guilty, and on the other, she had also represented a drug addict who she felt needed help instead of a lengthy prison sentence. "I wanted a job where I got thanked every once in a while," she says.

When Chávez's case file came to Ciuffini, she looked closely at the investigation that Deputy Sheriff Zúñiga had done. Ciuffini remembers thinking that in her experience, people didn't tend to make up incidents like the one Chávez described. She was also struck by the fact that since both Chávez and the supervisor confirmed that they had never met before, there wasn't an obvious motive for Chávez to lie about being the victim of such a serious crime. The suspect's statements to the police struck her, too. "He kept changing his story," Ciuffini says.

Like Zúñiga, she needed to make sure that she truly believed Chávez's account before taking up the case. To help Ciuffini decide, she asked an investigator from her office to arrange an interview with Chávez to see if holes and discrepancies in her story had reasonable explanations.

A few days later, Chávez arrived at the Kings County District Attorney's Office with Esmeralda Romero, a victim services advocate, who would help with Spanish-to-English interpretation. They were led to an interview room that had been purposely decorated to put visitors at ease.

Chávez was invited to sit on a couch, and Romero sat next to her. Ciuffini and Dennis Reed, the investigator, took armchairs opposite Chávez. Before beginning the interview, Reed set a tape recorder on the coffee table between them.

"We're at the Kings County District Attorney's Office with Guadalupe Chávez," Reed began. "We're gonna be speaking to you about an incident that happened to her out in, in Kettleman City. . . . We've read the report and actually the deputies did a good job on the report. But in reading it, we always have other questions to ask."

Ciuffini and Reed started by asking Chávez about her trip to get her overdue paycheck, the various stops that she and the supervisor had made during their drive. Then they started in on the sexual assault itself. How did the supervisor appear when he asked her for her underwear? "Like nervous, staring and looking all around," Chávez said.

Then they asked her to talk them through how she removed her underwear and why she did it. The interpreter translated: "She didn't want to make anything more difficult so she just went ahead and took off the underwear and gave 'em to him and she was

thinking in her head all he wants is my underwear, I may as well
give him my underwear and I'll get my check."

When he was penetrating her with his fingers, did she tell him
to stop? "No, she didn't," the interpreter said, translating. "She was
scared. She didn't think of anything. All she was thinking about is
if something happened to her, what were her kids gonna do?"

Next Reed and Ciuffini asked Chávez about the second assault.
"Okay I have to ask because somebody else is gonna ask if I don't,"
the investigator said. "When you got to that point and he was walking back with his pants unzipped, why didn't you drive away?"

Chávez spoke and the interpreter translated: "She didn't know
where she was going. That's why she thinks it's her fault because
she had time to go and get out of there and she didn't know any
roads where she was at. She didn't know."

"I understand, I do understand," the investigator said. "But I
need to ask, okay? But I understand you're lost. What were you
afraid of?"

"That he was gonna kill her or something was gonna happen,"
Chávez said through the interpreter.

"What did you think would happen to you if you said no?" Ciuffini asked.

"She doesn't know what would have happened but she knows
that she wouldn't be in all this mess. She said this is very embarrassing for her. She didn't want to say anything about it and she said
she's never told nobody about it . . . so this is very difficult for her."

Ciuffini had worked with enough victimized people to know
what her gut was telling her. She looked at the moon-faced woman
before her, her hair pulled back, the hurt and shame in her face.
The story stuck together. She believed Chávez.

If sexual assault and rape cases are rarely reported to the police,
then even fewer of them move forward through the criminal courts.
According to the Rape, Abuse & Incest National Network, the

country's largest organization working to reduce sexual violence, less than 4 percent of reported rapes and sexual assaults are taken up for prosecution, and only about half of those go to trial.[27]

The legal standard is necessarily high in these cases, and a prosecutor must prove beyond a reasonable doubt that the crime happened. Judges and juries must be sure that the defendant is responsible before finding guilt, because aside from prison time, a sex-crime conviction—which may require inclusion in a sex-offender registry—has long-term effects on job and housing opportunities. In more than two dozen states, convicted sex offenders face housing restrictions that could bar them from living near schools, parks, or other places where children are likely to visit.[28] This has led to increased homelessness and instability for convicted sex offenders, which also makes it difficult for them to find work and reintegrate into their communities, which in turn could make it more likely that they will reoffend.[29]

And wrongful convictions happen. Between 2012 and 2016, there have been at least sixty wrongful convictions based on sexual assault charges nationwide.[30]

The weight of a sex-crime conviction, coupled with the persistence of rape myths, makes sexual assault cases among the hardest cases to take to court, prosecutors say. "You have victims who are terrified of the process and they should be, frankly, because the system is largely intended to give the benefit of the doubt to the accused," says Joshua Marquis, the district attorney in Oregon who is also a spokesperson for the National District Attorneys Association.

Of the hundreds of felony cases he has taken to trial, the rape cases are the hardest, he adds. "The ones I remember the names of, the ones where I've stayed in touch with the victims, are the rape cases I've lost," he says. "They stay with me. They are more difficult to do than homicide cases. Because the victims survive."

For prosecutors, the decision to pursue these cases can be fraught, and they are not immune to political considerations. Almost all of the more than 2,300 local prosecutors in the United States are elected, and both the public and the criminal justice system itself tend to evaluate their performance based on their conviction rates.[31] Studies have found that prosecutors are sensitive to reelection and have been found to be more aggressive about taking on cases prior to an election.[32] At the same time, concerns around politics and public perception make some prosecutors hesitant to take on cases that they believe are unlikely to result in a conviction—including sexual assault cases, which are uniquely difficult to prosecute because victims are traumatized and vulnerable, and the crime itself is widely misunderstood by juries and the public.[33]

In a 2017 report aimed at upending the tendency of prosecutors to make decisions based on conviction rates, a group of criminal justice policy and training organizations argued that "conviction rates tell only part of the story about whether a prosecutor's office—or a prosecutor—is successful in handling cases involving sexual violence."[34]

"If difficult or challenging cases fall by the wayside early in the process, they are generally not factored into the rate of conviction," says the report, which was authored by three policy and training organizations: AEquitas, the Justice Management Institute, and the Urban Institute. "While there may be a thin veneer of success in terms of conviction rate, the reality is that serial perpetrators, or those who are clever in their choice of victim, escape justice, while victims who have been violated in the most personal and devastating way are left to their own remedies, without the support of the criminal justice system."

In an effort funded by the U.S. Department of Justice's Office on Violence Against Women, these three groups have advanced and will implement a new model for sexual assault prosecutions in a handful of jurisdictions across the country, one that emphasizes how cases are handled instead of conviction rates.[35]

For prosecutors, there has historically been little choice but to play to conviction rates or ignore them altogether. "I think that there are two basic competing philosophies about how prosecutors approach a decision about when to take a case, particularly a sex crimes case," says Alice Vachss, the former New York City prosecutor who has been critical of the way the criminal justice system handles sexual abuse. "One theory, and the one I believe in, is that you don't worry about conviction rates. Your job as a prosecutor is to go after the bad guys. The other competing theory is that you look at the likelihood of conviction and that is a big part of your prosecutorial decision."

In Hennepin County, Minnesota, County Attorney Mike Freeman says he is duty bound to take the probability of a trial win into account when deciding which cases to prosecute. Freeman had the power in 2008 to decide whether to pursue a criminal case on behalf of Leticia Zúñiga, a janitor who was undocumented at the time and who said she was raped while working as a cleaner at a shopping mall in suburban Minneapolis.

Zúñiga, who is not related to the deputy sheriff in California, says she had been raped after her supervisor called her into his subterranean office at the mall one afternoon.[36] After he shut the door, he told her to take off her clothes. She refused, but he forced her to have sex with him. That was the first of three rapes in his office, Zúñiga says. She adds that a fourth assault at the loading docks caused her so much pain that she ended up going to the hospital.

She says the supervisor, a man named Marco González, had pressured her to stay quiet by threatening to report her to immigration authorities. For months, she hadn't said a word to anyone, not even her husband. Holding such a dark secret had taken its toll. She barely ate, and when she was home, she avoided her family and hid in a bedroom. "I felt very closed in a world where I could not speak," she says.

For months, she lived through the torment alone. She couldn't stop working because her family relied on her paycheck and she knew it would be hard to find a new job without papers. She also didn't know what she would tell her husband if she quit. Mostly, she worried that González would report her to immigration if she spoke out against him because what scared her most was the idea of being separated from her two sons, who had both been born in the United States.

At work, Zúñiga says González alternated between physically attacking her and publicly chastising her in front of other workers. He called her a prostitute and a monkey, and he pointed out deficiencies in her work. Though she had every intention of keeping the assaults to herself, the public insults pushed her over the edge. A few months later, she quit and told her husband everything. "You have no idea how much it hurt me, and I could not believe that all of this was happening to me," Zúñiga says. "It hurt me a lot—so much that I got up the courage to talk."

Zúñiga and her husband went looking for help. They met with a worker advocacy organization that helped Zúñiga report what had happened to the mall management. The mall contacted SMS, the cleaning company that had employed Zúñiga. The company responded by asking González to investigate the problem himself.

The advocates also connected the janitor with free legal help from the University of Minnesota's law school. Lisa Stratton, a lawyer teaching at the school, oversaw a crew of law students who prepared a civil sexual harassment lawsuit against the janitorial company on Zúñiga's behalf. The lawsuit said that the company had failed to take her complaint seriously and hadn't created a clear-cut way for workers like Zúñiga to make a sexual harassment complaint.

As the civil case progressed, Stratton also encouraged Zúñiga to think about reporting the rapes to the police because it could give the janitor a chance at a special visa, known as a U visa, for noncitizen victims of crime who assist with the investigation or prosecution of crimes such as domestic violence, sexual assault, and human trafficking. Congress created the U visa program in 2000, and it requires an endorsement from law enforcement or a government official that states that the victim had been helpful in pursuing a criminal case.

In the spring of 2008, nearly a year after the final rape, Zúñiga summoned the courage to go to the police department. After she made her report, the police tried to gather DNA evidence by taking swab samples from González's office because Zúñiga said that the violent rape had led her to bleed on the carpet. She also said González had ejaculated onto the floor.

In conducting its investigation, the police spoke with González multiple times. Each time, his story shifted. In their first meeting, González denied any physical contact with Zúñiga. In the second, after he learned that the police were looking for DNA evidence, González told the police that Zúñiga had instigated things by kissing him and then masturbating him. He also told the police detective handling his case that his doctor could provide him with documentation that said that he was incapable of rape because he had erectile dysfunction.

Zúñiga's criminal case received some corroboration when Karla Perez, another janitor who had worked for SMS, came forward to say that she had been sexually assaulted by González, too. Perez had heard about Zúñiga's report, and it gave her the push she needed to make a complaint to the police.

The DNA testing that the police conducted was inconclusive, but based on the reports of Zúñiga and Perez, the police referred the rape charges against González to County Attorney Freeman for prosecution.

Freeman reviewed the case personally and decided that his

office would not move forward with prosecuting the case. "We had a strong report, the woman victim recounted the number of episodes and abuse she suffered," Freeman recalls. "Immediately we began to look for what we call 'hard evidence.' Where's the physical evidence? Is there a sexual assault kit? Do we have his sperm? Do we have other bodily fluids? Do we have eyewitnesses? Do we have camera surveillance? And unfortunately and tragically in this case all we had basically was her word and his word. We really didn't have hard evidence."

The lawyers handling Zúñiga's civil sexual harassment case, however, doggedly went in search of more physical evidence and corroboration. They found additional women who said that González had sexually harassed them. They learned that González had remodeled his office and changed the carpets before his office could be swabbed for DNA. They discovered that he had installed cameras and secretly recorded conversations with other workers as he fished for gossip on Zúñiga. Her lawyers, who were now working for a legal aid group called Gender Justice, also sought access to the supervisor's computer, a process that took close to two years. A forensics scrub of the computer in González's office showed that he went to websites like www.freerapepics.us.

Though the criminal case had been dropped, González was still being questioned by the U.S. Equal Employment Opportunity Commission in the civil case. He continued to offer disjointed and incompatible accounts of what had happened in his office with Zúñiga. In sworn testimony that he gave during the civil lawsuit, he said that despite what he had said to the police, he and Zúñiga had never had sexual relations. When Zúñiga's lawyer asked why he had told the police that he and the janitor had a consensual sexual relationship, he said that he had lied to law enforcement out of fear.

After five years of litigation, Zúñiga's sexual harassment case was settled in 2012. The company paid a settlement and didn't admit any wrongdoing. It also agreed to make changes to its sexual harassment policy, including implementing annual training for all of its workers and posting a human resources hotline so workers know whom to call if they have a problem. González, who was named in the civil suit, also settled the case without admitting liability, and continues to deny that he raped Zúñiga.

Two years after the civil case was settled, County Attorney Freeman said he still believes he made the right decision by turning Zúñiga's case away. Even with the additional circumstantial evidence that Zúñiga's attorneys turned up, there simply wasn't enough for him to bring a criminal case. "I think all of the additional facts, cameras in his office, porn on his computer, changing of carpet, implied or gave some evidence that he may well have done the crime or altered what happened, but that isn't enough hard evidence," Freeman says. "We gotta have bodily fluids, we gotta have eyewitnesses, we gotta have video cameras, we have to have him talking to other people about it."

Prosecutors like Kathy Ciuffini or Alice Vachss would disagree, but Freeman argues that it was, in fact, his ethical obligation to *not* prosecute Zúñiga's case. "Unfortunately, although we believe the crime was perpetrated, we couldn't prove it beyond a reasonable doubt," he says. "And we would be wrong in taking that case to trial."

In 2007, Guadalupe Chávez's case went to a criminal jury trial. Nearly everyone who had been in contact with Chávez about what had happened in the orchard was asked to testify: Senior Deputy Sheriff Kristopher Zúñiga and his investigation partner, district attorney investigator Dennis Reed, Alegria de la Cruz of the California Rural Legal Assistance, and Fabby Martínez, the medical assistant from the Corcoran District Hospital. Chávez also offered emotional testimony.

The accused supervisor did not take the witness stand, but the defense attorney raised various questions about Chávez's claims. Memorably, he argued that the sexual encounters couldn't have happened in the way that Chávez described because it would have been physically impossible for the supervisor, who is five-feet-four-inches tall, to have received a blow job from Chávez while she was seated in her car.

The defense attorney also introduced doubt about Chávez's character and her motivations. The fact that she had made a sexual harassment claim against another supervisor was used to make the point that Chávez was perhaps overly enthusiastic about filing complaints.

She also did not behave in the way a true victim does, the defense attorney said. Why hadn't she just driven away if she felt threatened in the orchard? Why didn't she seek help from a rape crisis center soon after the incidents if she had actually been assaulted? Why was the first person that she talked to about the rape her lawyer and not a friend or family member?

The defense pointed out that there had also been inconsistencies, big and small, related to Chávez's claims that he said ought to throw her credibility into question. For example, she had testified that the supervisor's pants had been unzipped but she had previously told the police that they were unbuttoned. She reported to the police that she had talked to the supervisor on her cell phone as they drove, but she also told attorney Alegria de la Cruz that there was no cell phone reception in the orchard. She said that he ejaculated on the side of her face during police questioning but testified in court that he had finished in her mouth. The defense attorney said that these are not inconsistencies that can be chalked up to trauma.

Taken together, Chávez simply shouldn't be believed, the defense attorney said. "It's too easy, as the lacrosse players at Duke University found out, to be accused," he said during his closing arguments. "It's too easy for our sons, nephews, grandsons to be accused of a sexual crime against a woman when it's her word versus his word."

In the end, almost everything about Guadalupe Chávez's case was an anomaly. She went to the police to report a rape. The local prosecutor agreed to take her case even though there was no witness and not much physical evidence.

In one key respect, however, Chávez's case did follow a common pattern: The jury found the accused supervisor not guilty. The verdict was consistent with national trends: about 2 percent of reported rape cases result in a felony conviction.[37]

In the years since trying the case, Ciuffini has reflected on the things she could have done as a prosecutor to bolster Chávez's case. She wonders if sending Chávez's clothes for DNA testing would have swayed the jury, though at the time, she thought it would be too expensive for too little gain, because the supervisor was arguing that the encounter had been consensual. Ciuffini says that it's common knowledge that sexual assault cases without a confession or clear-cut physical evidence are hard to win. It's why so many prosecutors are loath to bring them.

Ciuffini files them anyway, because "it's what the victim deserves," she says: "If they are brave enough to come forward and to testify in a jury trial, then I am willing to prosecute the case." She says she filed the case on behalf of Chávez because she believed her: "Because Guadalupe has a voice and she wanted it prosecuted and why should I make a decision for her?"

"I told her all the time, 'Guadalupe, I believe you,'" Ciuffini continues. "They said 'not guilty' but I believe you. You told your story and you were brave. What if you had let him get away with this and you didn't report it? He's on notice now.'"

These days, Chávez lives in a yellow mobile home in the Pacific Northwest that she bought after spending years working in the fields and in a Mexican food factory. Her sons are nearly grown.

She regularly attends an evangelical church where she covers her head with a scarf to demonstrate her humility before God and sings hymns loudly and with gusto.

She is now able to travel between the United States and Mexico on religious pilgrimages because she is on the route to citizenship, having earned a U visa for victims of crime after cooperating with Zúñiga and Ciuffini.

Reflecting on the arc of her case more than five years after the trial while seated at her dining room table, Chávez said she does not regret reporting the crime. Although her supervisor was acquitted, she says she has found some justice in the fact that he had to face a public confrontation from both her and the state of California. "At least that person will think twice before doing that," she said. "For that person, it was a warning—Hey, look, you can't do that anymore."

5

All That We Already Know

In October 1991, a thirty-five-year-old law professor named Anita Hill raised her right hand and swore to tell the truth at the confirmation hearing of Clarence Thomas, then a nominee to the U.S. Supreme Court.

With a gaggle of blinking TV cameras and the gaze of fourteen male senators from the Judiciary Committee fixed on her, Hill leaned into the microphone. She testified that while she had worked at the U.S. Department of Education and then later at the U.S. Equal Employment Opportunity Commission, Clarence Thomas had persistently asked her out on dates, discussed the content of the porn he had watched, and bragged about his sexual prowess.

"Because I was extremely uncomfortable talking about sex with him at all, and particularly in such a graphic way, I told him that I did not want to talk about these subjects," she said in an even, measured tone. "I would also try to change the subject to education matters or to nonsexual personal matters, such as his background or his beliefs. My efforts to change the subject were rarely successful."

No one had ever made such a public accusation of workplace sexual harassment before, and Hill closed her remarks by explaining why she had taken the unusual step of sharing her story. "I have no personal vendetta against Clarence Thomas," she said. "I seek only to provide the committee with information which it may regard as relevant. It would have been more comfortable to remain silent. I took no initiative to inform anyone. But when I was asked by a representative of this committee to report my experience, I felt that I had to tell the truth. I could not keep silent."

Hill's testimony was a watershed moment in the country's confrontation of sexual harassment in the workplace. A political commentator at the time called it a "national teach-in"; it catapulted the issue to greater national awareness and has had lasting and profound impact for America's working women.

In making explosive claims against such a prominent individual in such a public forum, Hill knew she would draw scrutiny and resistance. Thomas had categorically denied Hill's accusations, and he had decried the proceedings and argued that because he is an African American man, the entire affair had become a racialized circus. Though Hill is also African American, he famously described the confirmation process as a "high-tech lynching."[1] He said he was disgusted by the way that his good name and integrity had been tarnished by what he contended were Hill's baseless allegations.[2]

Hill offered historic testimony, but the process also devolved into a political soap opera that has generated unfortunate legacies. The tone and manner in which Hill was questioned reaffirmed a narrative that we have not entirely abandoned: Victims of sexual harassment—like victims of any kind of sexual violence—should expect to have their credibility questioned and their stories doubted.

The hearing was not meant to be a trial, though it was an overt effort to make a determination about Hill's allegations. The political stakes were high because White House officials under President George H.W. Bush had promised to advance a Supreme Court nominee who was "a true conservative," and the hearing was to assess whether Thomas, whom the administration favored, was fit to serve.[3]

Instead of one judge, Hill faced more than a half-dozen senators, some of whom were politically motivated to disbelieve her claims. The Republican senators who supported Thomas's confirmation were especially eager to discredit Hill. Through their questioning, they sought to minimize the harassment she described. They pressed her for explanations for incongruities in statements she had made to the press and the FBI, which later prompted Senator Arlen Specter to dismiss Hill's testimony as "flat-out perjury."[4]

Specter also suggested that her failure to report the harassment showed that Hill was making it up or exaggerating it. "How could you allow this kind of reprehensible conduct to go on right in the headquarters [of the U.S. Equal Employment Opportunity Commission], without doing something about it?" he demanded.

Hill responded with disarming calm:

> I can only say that when I made the decision to just withdraw from the situation and not press a claim or charge against him, that I may have shirked a duty, a responsibility that I had, and to that extent I confess that I am very sorry that I did not do something or say something, but at the time that was my best judgment. Maybe it was a poor judgment, but it wasn't dishonest and it wasn't a completely unreasonable choice that I made, given the circumstances.

Meanwhile, rumors swirled—some fed by the same Republican senators who doubted her story—that Hill was a lesbian and a scorned woman. Perhaps most outlandishly, she was accused of having erotomania, a delusion that Thomas was in love with her.[5]

Despite the efforts to question her credibility and her judgment, Hill was unimpeachable. She was poised and frank in her responses to the senators' questions. She passed a lie detector test.

Four friends—including an attorney, a law professor, and a judge—came forward to corroborate that Hill had confided in them about Thomas's behavior as it was happening.

Finally, for any who still deemed Hill unbelievable, another woman, Angela Wright, agreed to testify that she had also been sexually harassed by Thomas when she had worked for the U.S. Equal Employment Opportunity Commission.

In what has since been well documented in books, documentaries, newspaper articles, and even an HBO film, the Senate Judiciary Committee, seemingly driven by political considerations, decided to end the hearing after three days without calling Wright or additional witnesses on either side. Congress took up the matter two days later, confirming Thomas as an associate justice of the U.S. Supreme Court by four votes.

By questioning Hill's veracity so forcefully without giving her the chance to back up the weight of her claims, the senators sent a clear message that women who speak up about unwanted sexual behavior by a powerful man will be disbelieved and perhaps even publicly called liars.

Hill is aware of the hearing's unintended legacy. Reflecting on these events decades later, she said in interviews conducted in 2014 that the hearings were "unfair" and a "disservice to the public."[6] The committee asked "ill-informed questions" about the issue, she said, and "they were drawing on myths and things that had not been proven."[7]

The hearing helped cement the false idea that most sexual harassment cases are he-said she-said cases with no way to find the truth. Actually, there is usually more information that can be brought to bear. For example, in Hill's case, the committee could have called Angela Wright to testify about her allegations that Thomas had engaged in sexually inappropriate behavior at work. But it didn't. "The hearings showed people what happens when representatives don't make a real attempt to get to the bottom of issues and to understand how sexual harassment works," Hill said in a 2016 *Time* magazine interview.[8]

The hearings also reinforced an ongoing misconception that a true victim of sexual harassment or any sexual violence responds immediately and aggressively to the problem. This was a central theme that the committee used to question Hill's veracity. If it really happened, why didn't she do something about it?

The public also considered this discrediting. News polls taken during the hearing showed that most people didn't believe that Hill had been sexually harassed, partially because they thought that someone who had been harassed in this way would have said or done something forceful in response.[9]

In an October 1991 *USA Today* article, a Minneapolis focus group said that Hill should have been angrier and acted sooner.[10] A female marketing consultant told the newspaper, "Something's not clicking. From a female point of view, I cannot understand why the relationship continued in any form."

Hill's testimony did prompt a noticeable rise in sexual harassment reporting to the federal government, but the idea that "real victims" of harassment or violence automatically respond aggressively and report it is a stubborn and widely held assumption that received a boost from the Thomas confirmation hearing. It does not, however, square with reality. In fact, decades of empirical research dating back to the 1980s tells us that the exact opposite is true.

In 1981, nearly a decade before Clarence Thomas's confirmation hearing, the federal government published the country's first survey on sexual harassment, conducted by the Merit Systems Protection Board, a quasi-judicial federal agency created to protect U.S. government employees from unfair and arbitrary treatment. The report was titled "Sexual Harassment in the Federal Workplace: Is It a Problem?" The board surveyed about twenty thousand employees of the federal government and concluded that unwanted sexual behavior at work was, in fact, "widespread" and "an important concern in the workplace."

The study also noted that workers tended not to report the problem, and when they did, many found that speaking up either didn't help or made things worse. "This indicates that much still needs to be done to make supervisors and other officials accountable for resolving these problems informally," the report says.

It was a crucial study issued at a moment when sexual harassment was emerging as an increasingly urgent issue. In 1979, a few years before the federal government study was released, a legal scholar named Catharine MacKinnon published a seminal book, *Sexual Harassment of Working Women: A Case of Sex Discrimination*. It documented the impact of sexual harassment on female workers and argued that sexual harassment was illegal because it is a form of sex discrimination prohibited by Title VII of the U.S. Civil Rights Act of 1964.

The book also advanced the idea that there are different types of sexual harassment, such as ongoing verbal and physical behavior that creates a hostile work environment, as opposed to "quid pro quo" harassment, whereby victims are coerced into unwanted sexual contact or activity. The legal analysis proposed by MacKinnon in *Sexual Harassment of Working Women* was eventually adopted by the U.S. Supreme Court in 1986 with its decision in *Meritor Savings Bank v. Vinson*.

The federal case centered around allegations made by Mechelle Vinson, a bank employee, who said that, among other things, she had been raped by her immediate supervisor. He denied the allegations, and the bank argued that Vinson did not notify them of the problem. The bank won at trial, but Vinson won on appeal, and the U.S. Supreme Court agreed to hear the case.

MacKinnon was one of the attorneys representing Vinson, and the high court's resulting decision is significant because it established general guidelines for judging sexual harassment claims, making it clear that a hostile work environment—in addition to quid pro quo harassment—is illegal under federal civil rights law. This legal framework remains in place today.

As these types of critical legal and cultural questions around sexual harassment were being raised with great energy and attention in the mid-1980s, Louise Fitzgerald was an assistant professor of psychology in Ohio. As a feminist who had studied women's history, Fitzgerald understood immediately that harassment was a significant barrier to women in the workplace. She had read with great interest *The Lecherous Professor: Sexual Harassment on Campus*, a book published in 1984 that examined sexual harassment in higher education through various case studies.

Fitzgerald was struck by the stories of harassment in the book. When a federal grant opportunity came up, she decided to study the issue using her training in statistical analysis, drafting a research proposal aimed at figuring out how to quantify sexual harassment. "People talked about it but no one really knew how to really measure it," Fitzgerald recalls. "No one knew how much of it there was, and even what it is."

When she was awarded the grant, in 1984, Fitzgerald assembled an all-female research team. In those early days, there was no common understanding of what could be deemed sexual harassment, so the group's first task was to create a survey questionnaire that would more fully capture women's experience with the problem. The team called the survey the Sexual Experiences Questionnaire, or the SEQ.[11]

"The research was such a riot," Fitzgerald recalls. "We were in our lab writing items for the SEQ, and we'd name them for the people that did those things. There was the 'John Brant Memorial Item' because he would come up behind you and put his arm around you. There was the 'Andy Jones Memorial Item.' Every one of those items was written from real-life experience."[12]

The team tested the SEQ on two college campuses to see which questions worked and which did not. They made adjustments and refinements, and today the SEQ has become the go-to questionnaire for measuring sexual harassment. A significant body of research has shown that it works well, though some business-school scholars have criticized it for overestimating sexual harassment because it uses a social science conception of the issue instead of the legal definition. The questionnaire is widely used by researchers all over the world.[13]

Fitzgerald says the SEQ was novel then and remains relevant now because it doesn't treat sexual harassment as a singular event. Instead, sexual harassment is seen as the sum of a range of behaviors over time that constitutes unwanted sexual attention.

In addition to helping define what sexual harassment is, the SEQ also explores how people respond to it. The questionnaire asks whether the victim of sexual harassment reported the problem and if not, why not? If the person did, what happened?

From the pilot test of the SEQ, the researchers found strong indications that, contrary to popular belief, most women did not report harassment because they didn't know where to report it and because they were afraid to make a complaint. "The main thing was fear," Fitzgerald says. "The fear of not being believed, afraid of being retaliated against and getting in trouble, and feeling embarrassed."

Though these findings were in line with the federal government's survey from 1981, it contradicted a line of academic studies of sexual harassment that found that women *said* they were likely to report sexual harassment and that they would respond aggressively to put an end to it.[14]

These studies had reach, and they fed the faulty assumption that true victims would naturally take swift and strong action in response to sexual harassment. However, this so-called perceptions research had a significant methodological flaw. It was purely theoretical, based on the opinions of college students presented with hypothetical scenarios in a psychology lab.

Fitzgerald did one study using this approach, but she quickly saw its limitations: "They are very easy to do, because you write a little story on a piece of paper, and you get a bunch of college students to read it, and they say, 'Well this is what I would do if this happened to me.' What we have come to find out is, it's [much more] difficult to sit in a safe classroom and read a story and speculate about what you would realistically do under the circumstances than it is to actually do those things when he comes up behind you and grabs you."

The spuriousness of this research was clearly shown in a study where women at a university were asked how they would respond to harassment.[15] Next, they underwent an interview that they did not know was related to the study. To measure how the same subjects would *actually* respond to unwanted sexual attention, the male interviewer purposely asked a series of unseemly personal and sexual questions. In the end, researchers found that few of the participants challenged the inappropriate questions—even the women who had said that they would respond aggressively to sexual harassment in the first part of the study.

Driven by the responses from the pilot study of the SEQ, Fitzgerald and her colleagues began to prepare additional studies to look more specifically at how women respond to sexual harassment. But first, she got a surprising phone call. A former graduate student's aunt was working on the legal team of a law professor named Anita Hill, who was preparing to testify about sexual harassment in conjunction with the Clarence Thomas confirmation hearing. Hill's legal team learned of Fitzgerald's work, and they asked if she would help put Hill's claims in context by presenting what she had learned in the process of creating and testing the SEQ.

Fitzgerald agreed, although she was never called to testify. The sexual harassment researcher became one of the witnesses, along with Angela Wright and Thomas's expert witness, who were fore-closed from making public remarks. Nevertheless, the experience offered Fitzgerald a live case study about the vast misconceptions the public had about how people respond to sexual harassment.

Fitzgerald watched from the hearing room as Hill's credibility and even her sanity were questioned, and she learned contemporaneously of the death threats that the law professor was receiving. "I was appalled by the whole thing," Fitzgerald says. "It played out exactly how sexual harassment plays out when a woman makes a claim against a powerful man. Anita's was a classic case and there was nothing unusual about it at all except that it played out on a national stage."

Hill's treatment at the confirmation hearing underscored the gap between what sexual harassment victims believed was a realistic response and what was expected of them. After the hearings ended, Fitzgerald joined some pro-Anita rallies in Washington, D.C., and then she went back to work.

In 1995, she and a few colleagues published a paper in the *Journal of Social Issues* that provided a direct response to those who had misunderstood Anita Hill. It was titled "Why Didn't She Just Report Him? The Psychological and Legal Implications of Women's Responses to Sexual Harassment," and it opened with an examination of the public's disbelief of Hill's testimony.[16] The researchers reviewed the studies that had been done in the intervening years and found widespread agreement that for most victims, addressing the sexual harassment directly through formal complaints or lawsuits was a "last resort when all other efforts have failed."

Victims of sexual harassment were understandably dissuaded from reporting because they knew that, in the rare instances when someone made a formal complaint or filed a lawsuit, they faced consequences like workplace retaliation, losing their job, or social ostracism. In other words, Fitzgerald and her colleagues found, "Despite pervasive public opinion that women should 'handle' harassment assertively, confront the perpetrator immediately, and report him to appropriate authorities, reactions to such responses are generally not favorable for those who actually 'blow the whistle.'"

This situation has not improved. According to representatives of the U.S. Equal Employment Opportunity Commission, sexual harassment claims have become more extreme and tend to involve claims of retaliation. Anna Park, a regional attorney for the commission, said that she has observed that "as the years passed, the severity of the harassment became worse."

"What started out as verbal comments, maybe graffiti in the bathrooms, we started seeing over time more physical aggressive harassment—women being forced to have sex, giving oral sex, raped, subjected to sexual battery," she says.[17] She adds that workers in low-wage industries such as food service, agriculture, and night-shift janitorial work have been particularly susceptible to these types of abuses, and she has handled a number of these kinds of cases for the government.

But the research that observed that sexual harassment victims tended to not report the problem did not simultaneously find that victims simply did nothing in response to the harassment. "It's not that women are passive," Fitzgerald says. "That's what we were so struck by. They were very much trying to actively manage the situation based on the options they had available to them and what made sense to them. They don't do nothing. They just don't do what people on the outside think they should be doing, and they don't do it for very good reasons."

Most victims managed the problem in a range of quotidian and practical ways. Some avoided the perpetrator. Some tried to deflect advances by offering excuses or making jokes. Some coped with the situation by telling themselves that the harassment wasn't really a problem, or that it was unintentional, or that perhaps it was their fault and they had invited it. But most frequently the women "simply endure, hoping that the situation will eventually go away without the embarrassment and retaliation that so often accompany a formal complaint," the researchers wrote.

By studying the coping strategies of sexual harassment victims, Fitzgerald and her collaborators found that women were making complex calculations about how to respond. And because harassment may be ongoing or may escalate, Fitzgerald and her colleagues described the decision about whether or not to report or complain as being part of an ongoing decision-making process. "Such evaluations are part of a complex, reflexive process that changes over time as the situation unfolds," the researchers wrote.[18]

Since then, many studies involving various populations and professions have found that it is often unreasonable to expect sexual harassment victims to report the problem to management or the government.[19] In 2002, Fitzgerald joined Mindy Bergman, Lilia Cortina, and others considered among the foremost researchers on sexual harassment, to conduct an oft-cited large-scale study that looked at how women in the U.S. military respond to sexual harassment.[20] It gave yet more credence to what Fitzgerald and others had seen in prior studies.

The researchers surveyed more than 28,000 members of the military. They found that the approximately 6,000 people who said they had been sexually harassed reported lower job satisfaction and increased psychological distress, but a majority had not reported the harassment to their superiors, and those who did found that it often resulted in some form of retaliation. As the researchers wrote, "Such results suggest that, at least in certain work environments, the most 'reasonable' course of action for the victim is to avoid reporting."

Even cases of extreme sexual harassment—such as sexual assault or rape by co-workers and supervisors—do not consistently result in high rates of reporting or inspire aggressive responses. A 2013 study of sexual harassment among law enforcement, by End Violence Against Women International and other groups, found that unwanted physical touching by supervisors prompted 8 percent of police officers to file a formal complaint. When their coworkers tried to force them into sex, the officers in the study *never* made complaints. The researchers also found that although most of the participants in their study had experienced behaviors that could potentially be considered sexual harassment, "very few were reported with a formal complaint, but retaliation was common and often severe."[21] Indeed, retaliation included delays in assistance from their coworkers during emergency situations and tampering with safety equipment.

Another study from 1991 explored the dynamics around workplace sexual assault among nearly four hundred professional women from the East Coast.[22] About 17 percent reported that someone they knew from work had either sexually assaulted them or tried to. People in supervisory positions were behind nearly half of the incidents, which tended to involve more extreme behavior. However, making a formal complaint was found to be complicated by the fact that the supervisors made economic and physical threats against—or job-related promises to—their victims. In general, the study found, "The assailant was a person with legitimate, institutionalized means to alter a woman's working or learning conditions or the assailant used intrusive physical actions or both."

Given these dynamics, the professional East Coast women in the study did not often quit or even complain after being harassed or attacked. About 80 percent of them stayed in their jobs after a workplace assault, and nearly 70 percent continued to report to the same person who had abused them. "Women who quit did not lodge a complaint; women who lodged a complaint did so for the most part in those rare instances in which an outsider was the assailant," the study says. "Daily workplace interactions no doubt continued unchanged on the surface, while the woman worker adjusted to her situation unaided by interpersonal or institutional support."

If reporting is uncommon in general, then for immigrant women in low-wage industries who face additional practical barriers to reporting sexual harassment, it is even rarer. As Fatima Goss Graves of the education and workplace-equity organization National Women's Law Center put it in 2015 testimony before the U.S. Equal Employment Opportunity Commission, "For migrant workers who are harassed, seeking justice can mean risking their livelihoods, putting their families at risk and potentially facing deportation," she said.

There appears to be little benefit for anyone—especially an immigrant woman working for meager pay in agricultural, janitorial, or domestic work—to aggressively resist and report sexual harassment. Yet, as the Clarence Thomas confirmation hearings established, the courts and the public seem to expect sexual harassment victims to act against their own interests.

As Fitzgerald and other scholars studied how women respond to and cope with sexual harassment, there were academics looking at the problem from the other side of the equation. They asked different but related questions: Who are the men most likely to sexually abuse women? If there are ways to pinpoint these tendencies, are there ways to intervene?

This line of research began with Neil Malamuth, who in the late 1960s was an ambitious undergraduate at UCLA with plans to become a high-powered lawyer. Malamuth, now a psychology professor at his alma mater, was diverted from his legal aspirations when he stumbled across an ad for a research-assistant job in the university's psychology department. He soon found himself working on an experiment exploring the connection between sex and aggression toward women. As the newly minted research assistant, it was his job to pretend to receive electrical shocks from the participants of the study while sitting in another room. Malamuth found the job terribly boring, but it ushered him onto a new academic path.

Malamuth began conducting psychological research on risk taking and conflict resolution, though he couldn't help but stay attuned to the discussions on feminism and women's rights that were raging around him on campus. He found the debates around the eroticization of violence against women in ads and pop culture particularly compelling. From shoe designers to rock bands, it had become common for female corpses or women's bruised bodies to be used to market products and brands. "Some people were saying that this is fantasy and everyone knows that this is a chic way of getting attention and it doesn't affect people's real attitudes or behaviors," Malamuth says of the debate that was happening at the time. "Other people were saying, 'No. This is both a reflection of the problem and a cause.'"

Malamuth wanted to get to the bottom of things, so he came up with an experiment. He would randomly assign male participants into two groups. One would read a sexually violent story from a porn magazine, and another group would read the same story with all of the violent passages removed. Then he would use a survey to gauge whether the material made them feel more aggressive toward women.

The researcher was days away from starting the experiment when he found himself on campus talking to some friends. A woman walked by and she caught the attention of one of the men in the group. After she had moved on, one of the men said, "If I could get away with it, I'd jump her." No one in the group blinked at the comment. Instead, they all stood there, nodding their heads.

Malamuth was struck by the whole scene, and before running his experiment, he added a final question to the survey: "If you knew you were assured that you would not be caught or punished, would you force a woman to have sex with you?"

Malamuth's study, published in 1980, didn't find much evidence that a single exposure to sexually violent content from a porn magazine had much influence on men's sexual aggression toward women one way or the other.[23] However, the question that he had thrown in at the last minute drew an astonishing response. One third of the participants said that they would probably force a woman into sex acts if they knew they wouldn't get caught.

Malamuth decided to look more closely at that group of men, a segment of the respondents that he described as having a "high likelihood to rape" compared to the others. Among the other questions he had asked in his survey, Malamuth looked for trends and commonalities among those who said that they would rape a woman if they knew they could get away with it.

He found that the men who had a proclivity to rape tended to have more callous attitudes toward sexual assault in general, and they were more likely to believe in myths about rape, including the notion that women secretly enjoy it. He also found that this group of men were more likely to be sexually aroused by depictions of rape.

Through additional research, he pinpointed two general frameworks to describe the characteristics of men who admitted to committing acts of violent aggression against women but who had never been convicted. First, this group tended to have individual experiences that led them to decontextualize sex from a relationship. Second, they had been socialized into and accepted ideas of male dominance.[24]

To further test these ideas, Malamuth conducted a study to compare convicted rapists in prison to the men who said they would rape if they knew they wouldn't get caught. After giving the study participants a diagnostic test, Malamuth compared the results to the preexisting academic literature on the characteristics of rapists. He found that on almost every condition, men who said they would force a woman to have sex if they could get away with it were similar to those who had been convicted of the crime. Specifically, both of these groups tended to be more accepting of violence against women and to view sex outside the context of a relationship. The only finding that surprised Malamuth was that convicted rapists were not necessarily more hostile toward women than the likely-to-rape men.[25]

The strength of the likely-to-rape framework has since been borne out in numerous studies by other scholars, and in particular a 1995 study that Malamuth conducted gave it additional reliability.[26] With National Institute of Mental Health funding, Malamuth and his colleagues reconnected with a group of Canadian men who had taken his survey on sexual aggression toward women decades before as college students. He followed up to see how they had fared.

Malamuth located these former students, who were now in their early thirties, to gauge whether they had, in fact, acted in sexually aggressive ways. Based on reports from both the ex-students and their romantic partners at the time, the study found that those who had scored high in sexual aggression in their youth were more likely to engage in verbal abuse and aggressive behavior toward their partners as adults.

Malamuth says that, taken as a whole, his research has shown that male attraction to sexual violence is more common than most people had previously realized. "Aggression against women is not the product of a sick, abnormal man," Malamuth says. "The potential for it is embedded in the culture. Culture can affect it, if they are given permission."

Malamuth's work is what paved the way for similar research on workplace sexual harassment. In the late 1980s, at about the same time Louise Fitzgerald was testing the Sexual Experiences Questionnaire on women, a psychologist at Illinois State University named John B. Pryor began to adapt Malamuth's ideas about the likelihood to rape to concepts of sexual harassment.

Pryor focused on the more extreme and coercive types of sexual harassment in the workplace, such as quid pro quo harassment. Borrowing from Malamuth, Pryor developed a Likelihood to Sexually Harass scale by asking men how likely they were to engage in a series of ten hypothetical scenarios if they were assured that there would be no consequences for their actions.[27] One question, for example, asked whether the participant would give a woman a promotion in exchange for sexual favors if they knew they would never get caught.

The study participants were then given additional surveys, including the sexual aggression questionnaires that Malamuth had designed to examine men's likelihood to rape. Finally, they were asked to participate in an exercise that would test their treatment of women.

Taking these things together, Pryor found that those who were likely to sexually harass tended to hold adversarial sexual beliefs, to have higher rape proclivities, to find it hard to see other people's points of view, to be more authoritarian, and to subscribe to rigid sex roles. The Likelihood to Sexually Harass scale, known as the LSH, has since been widely adopted and translated into various languages for use in other countries.

Pryor says that the research into men who are likely to sexually harass reveals that "sex and power are cognitively connected in the minds of people who are likely to commit sexually coercive acts by their own admission."

As a result, certain jobs and work environments are particularly conducive to creating the kind of power imbalances that make undocumented workers easy targets, he says. "Immigrants, particularly illegal immigrants, have a long history of being in the situation where they are being extorted by employers, sometimes sexually," Pryor says.

Through the academic research, a possible solution began to emerge. In the early 1990s, a few years after Pryor piloted the LSH, one of Pryor's graduate students, Christine La Vite, conducted a pivotal study.[28] She assigned men who had scored both high and low on the LSH to participate in one of two staged scenarios in the lab: one in which an authority figure pretended to sexually harass a trainee and another in which the authority figure acted professionally toward a trainee. The participant was then asked to take over the training, and his behavior was observed.

The experiment produced an interesting discovery. The men who had scored high on the LSH were more likely to harass if the person demonstrating the training portion of the study had engaged in sexual harassment himself. The opposite was also true, however. Men who were inclined to sexually harass did less of it when the supervisor had acted professionally. "What it showed was that local norms as conveyed by a person in authority are important," Pryor says.

This finding has been replicated in additional research by Pryor. In one study from the mid-1990s, Pryor and his colleagues analyzed large-scale Department of Defense survey data.[29] They looked at the reports from the study participants in various offices of the department about whether or not they thought the local leadership was tolerant of sexual harassment. Then they examined the responses from the same offices about their experiences with sexual harassment. The study once again found that authority figures were influential. In the offices where workers reported high tolerance for sexual harassment, they also reported higher rates of experiencing it.

In another study, Pryor and his colleagues examined how social norms of groups can affect sexual harassment.[30] He recruited students and measured their LSH before bringing them into a laboratory setting. He put the participants into groups of three men based on their LSH scores. Three men who scored high on the scale were grouped together and three men with low scores were put together. Then Pryor gave the students a cover story. They were told that they were going to do a trust exercise by leading a blindfolded woman—a confederate who was also a researcher—around a maze. Each person in the group would take a turn as the leader.

"What we found was, of course, that the groups of men who were high on the Likelihood to Sexually Harass scale, in general, did more inappropriate touching then men who were low, who didn't do it all," Pryor says. Among the men who were likely to harass, Pryor also noticed a "cascading phenomenon." If the first person did something inappropriate, then it increased the likelihood that the second person would, too. If the first two behaved badly, then the third was very likely to, as well.

"My interpretation was that we were seeing the development of something analogous to local social norms," Pryor says. "People are influenced by what other people are doing."

These findings can have real-world application to the workplace and an actual effect on the prevalence of sexual harassment, he says. Sexual harassment can effectively be "short-circuited if someone in a leadership position says, 'This is not going to be tolerated,'" he says. "But often you have the development of norms from the ground up where you put together a bunch of guys who want to do this kind of thing and they will encourage each other."

Sexual harassment in many ways, then, is situational. "People who are likely to sexually harass are less likely to perform those behaviors in circumstances where there is a strong social pressure not to do it," Pryor says.

"Social pressure is a powerful force," he adds. "As human beings, our instincts are to go along with what others are doing. Sexual harassment is something that most people know that they shouldn't be doing, so it's about reinforcing that by creating social norms that say that this is not what you should be doing."

Though they had started on opposite sides of the question, Louise Fitzgerald and her colleagues looking at the problem from the victim's point of view had arrived at the same conclusion. In research that studied the "organizational factors" that led to sexual harassment, they found that work environment and the attitudes of their superiors had great impact.[31]

"That's one of the things we do know: If a company sends a strong message that it does not tolerate this behavior, there will be less sexual harassment," Fitzgerald says. "Some people will still act out, but there will be a lot less of it."

A formidable body of research has drawn similar conclusions, but even as it creates a path toward prevention, sexual harassment hasn't gone away. About 6,800 people reported being sexually harassed in the workplace to the federal government in 2016, and an unknown number experience it without ever saying a word about it.[32]

In other words, as a society, we have long known how to minimize sexual harassment. We have just not yet decided to do it.

6

The Ways Forward

It was a muggy May morning in 2016 when about fifty farmworkers, almost a dozen of them women, emerged from a retired school bus and shuffled into the hiring office of Pacific Tomato Growers in Palmetto, Florida. They had come directly from the fields, still wearing shade-bearing hats and bandanas, their sleeves freshly tinted a lime green from pulling the fruit from its leafy plants. Their shoes tracked a trail of dirt onto the industrial carpeting as they filed in to take seats in plastic chairs.

Angel García, the farm's upbeat human resources manager, stood near the door and greeted each attendee as if he were the host of a party. He shook hands, smiled broadly, and called out some longtime workers by name.

After everyone had sunk into their chairs, García set the stage. The workers were there for a new training program on workplace violence, he said. They were there to learn how to identify and report sexual harassment in the fields, and they would also get information about what to do if they or their coworkers were in abusive relationships.

"We started developing a training for farmworkers a long time ago as a way for them to understand harassment and violence in the workplace," García told the group in both Spanish and English.

For the next half hour, he said, the group would watch three short videos, and after each one, they would discuss what they had seen. He paused patiently between phrases as his words were translated into Creole for the Haitian workers in the crowd.

There was nothing particularly complicated about the training that García had described, and yet the fact that it was happening at all was revolutionary.

Workplace violence training for workers isn't common and is even more unusual when sexual violence and domestic violence are included in the conversation. What's more, in an industry where human resources departments are a rarity and the timing of production dictates everything, every one of the thousand workers at Pacific Tomato Growers Farm #1 was receiving workplace sexual violence training that week on company time in the middle of the harvest.

The training itself was novel because it wasn't a corporate training program that had been dubbed into Spanish and Creole. Instead, it had been designed by farmworkers for farmworkers with the goal of making it accessible in language and content for people who might be unaware that there were laws prohibiting sexual harassment, and who might not know what their options were if they were a victim of sexual assault or domestic abuse themselves.

This was a conscious decision by the group that had crafted the training, a collaboration among Florida farmworker advocacy organizations, like the Coalition of Immokalee Workers and the Fair Food Standards Council; employers, like Pacific Tomato; and Vida Legal Assistance, which is dedicated to assisting immigrant survivors of violence. These groups had been brought together by Futures Without Violence, an organization that has worked to counter gender-based violence for more than thirty years. In 2014, Futures Without Violence launched its Low Wage, High Risk project to address gender-based violence among vulnerable workers in three sites and industries scattered across the country. Pacific Tomato

Growers Farm #1 was one of them. In all three, the goal was to generate new approaches tailored to each industry.

"We want the workers to identify with the type of violence they are likely to see," says Ana Vallejo of Vida Legal Assistance. "The behavior is the same anywhere, but it looks different in the fields and the expression of it is different. Here, workers can see domestic violence and sexual violence examples that they can relate to."

Back in the hiring office, the lights faded. The first video featured a worker named Alicia, whose supervisor had tried to grab her in his truck and had stalked her outside of work. Alicia confided in a co-worker as she sat at a company lunch table, and she said she was afraid to report her supervisor's behavior because she didn't want to lose her job. Her co-worker showed her a list of phone numbers she could call to get help and assured Alicia that she had the right to make a complaint. The call could even be confidential if she liked.

Upbeat panpipe music closed out the scene, a signal that the first segment had come to a close. In the Pacific Tomato hiring office, the lights came back on. A human resources representative from the farm named Jessica Abrigo stood in front of the group. "Who can tell me in which ways the supervisor was inappropriate toward Alicia?" she asked.

The question was met with a few seconds of silence. Abrigo asked the question a different way: "What were the things that made Alicia worried about her supervisor?"

A male worker volunteered in Spanish that Alicia was afraid that the supervisor would fire her, which inspired one of the women in a pink baseball cap to jump in to concur. Their responses were translated from Spanish to English to Creole, which prompted a man wearing a black Superman cap to ask in Creole, "If this were to happen, what office would they go to? Because they are scared of the supervisor. He's the problem."

"This is a very good question," said García, the gregarious human resources rep. "We are going to clarify very quickly the levels of authority. If you go through that chain of command, everyone has the ability to address a problem with the person underneath them."

One of the collaborators in the training, Lindsay Adams, added that in addition to calling the company, they could also call her organization's twenty-four-hour confidential hotline. Workers have a right to complain, and the company cannot fire them for reporting a problem, said Adams, who is an inspector with the Fair Food Standards Council, a workers' rights organization.

"Your question was awesome," García told the worker in English. It was immediately translated into Creole and Spanish.

The lights dimmed again, and next came a video segment about a woman living in the company's farmworker housing with a verbally and physically abusive husband. When the clip had ended, the workers were led through another discussion. They were asked to think about the damaging effects of controlling and violent relationships, including their effects on the victims at work. The group was told that the company had developed a policy on domestic violence so workers can also go to the company for help.

The final segment tackled verbal sexual harassment. It began in the tomato fields with a woman walking past a worker named César. "Sexy mama!" he called out to her. "All those curves and me with no brakes! I'd love to take her home and have her make me tortillas."

The crowd had watched the first two segments in rapt silence but this exchange elicited chortles and giggles. It was all a little too real.

In the video, a coworker steps in and tells César to be respectful of the women he works with, but César is dismissive. "You have to show the woman who's the man," he replied. César's co-worker doesn't give him a pass but instead asks César if he would want his mother or sister treated the same way. The exchange gets César thinking and later, when other men catcall female workers, he can be seen moving along with his work without joining in.

When the lights came back on, the group was still laughing and shaking their heads. Julia de la Cruz, an organizer with the Coalition of Immokalee Workers, stood before the group to lead the discussion. A former farmworker, she had helped write the script and had acted the role of Alicia in the first segment. She had seen for herself what happens in the fields. "Everyone was laughing," she observed. "Is this something you see or not?"

With her question, the laughter fell off a cliff into a heavy silence. "If you see something like this, you shouldn't have fear speaking up," de la Cruz continued. "You should help out the other female workers. You should speak up; you shouldn't be afraid."

García picked up on an unspoken cue and returned to stand before the group. He had a tough question for the crowd: This is a problem not just for women but also for men, so why don't men say something to other men when they hear talk like this?

No answer.

García filled the silence by saying, "We are creating a culture of respect and one part of that is to challenge males to talk to other males."

The half hour was almost up. The workers were shown a list of phone numbers of organizations they could contact if they had a problem with sexual harassment or domestic violence. To conclude, Abrigo, the human resources staffer, asked the group if anyone had any final questions or comments.

The worker in the Superman cap who had been the first to speak rose from his seat. In Creole, he said, "Thank you for thinking of us with this video, and for the different ways to contact you if we were to have a problem or situation, to maintain a safe place to work."

Then just as swiftly as they had filed in, the workers were up and lined up at the door. There was a boisterous shuffle back to the buses as the workers prepared to return to the blazing heat of the tomato fields.

Over the course of a day and a half, the tomato pickers, planters,

and harvest dumpers from Pacific Tomato Growers Farm #1 were
bused in from the fields or farm housing to the hiring office. Each
group of fifty or sixty filed in and sat through the same thirty-
minute presentation.

In this way, the workers were shown how to identify the kinds
of sexual harassment or domestic violence that they might actually
see in their jobs. They were reminded of the resources available to
them, and they were assured that no one could be fired for raising
a problem with management.

With the final group of Pacific Tomato workers, García put a fine
point on the purpose of the training. "In two days, we trained the
entire farm so we can change the culture," he said. "So that nothing happens and if it does, you know you can report it. So that you
say, 'No, we will not be quiet.' One person can make a difference."

The efforts at Pacific Tomato differed from most sexual harassment training programs because they weren't happening in a vacuum. It followed an all-day training tailored for farm supervisors,
focusing on specific scenarios that were likely to crop up in an
agricultural setting. From there, the supervisors learned that it was
part of their job to address the problem, and they were shown, step
by step, what they could do to begin to resolve the issue.

For some field-level supervisors, this was a revelation about their
role in confronting sexual harassment. "There were supervisors
that said, 'I don't want to get involved,'" says Laura Safer Espinoza,
a retired New York State Supreme Court justice and the executive
director of the Fair Food Standards Council, which collaborated in
the training program. "And we started to make them understand
that you are responsible for the work environment."

The training itself was not the solution, however, and training
for training's sake doesn't seem to accomplish much. In 2015, the
U.S. Equal Employment Opportunity Commission, which upholds
the laws that protect workers from sexual harassment at work,
convened a Select Task Force on the Study of Harassment in the

Workplace. In an effort to find new strategies for tackling a long-standing problem, the group reviewed the research that evaluates sexual harassment training. It found that most of the existing studies have methodological deficiencies, but the handful of large-scale studies on the topic found that, while sexual harassment trainings can raise awareness, they don't always change worker attitudes on the issue.[1] One of these studies found that employees who had received training were more likely to report sexual harassment when the company communicates that it does not tolerate it. But when these researchers looked at whether training had an effect on the frequency of harassment that workers experienced, they found no evidence that it had.

"Training has become an activity that corporations undertake to protect themselves from liability," says Louise Fitzgerald, the professor emeritus with the University of Illinois at Urbana-Champaign who has conducted some of the foremost studies on sexual harassment. "The training itself is ineffective and counterproductive generally because a lawyer stands up and says 'Thou shalt not do this and thou shalt not do that.' Guys get defensive and it doesn't do anything.

"People don't do this stuff because they don't know it's wrong, which is the premise of current training," she continues. "We have to have a different focus for the training on how we need to treat women with respect. It needs to be more proactive rather than reactive."

The groups behind the training at Pacific Tomato were betting that it would have benefits precisely because it focused on changing workplace norms. As decades worth of research by Louise Fitzgerald and others has shown, when a company clearly communicates that sexual harassment is not tolerated, there is less of it. That was a key takeaway from the training in Florida—everyone at the farm had a responsibility to prevent sexual harassment from happening.

An organizational culture that repudiates sexual harassment also resonates with a growing consensus that onus of combating sexual harassment and assault cannot be placed only on the shoulders of victims. The research by Fitzgerald and others tells us that victims have a variety of valid reasons for not reporting the problem; when complaints are made, there can be negative consequences. "Going and making a complaint does not make things better and in some cases actually makes things worse," Fitzgerald says.

The U.S. Equal Employment Opportunity Commission task force was created out of the realization that the most common forms of recourse—complaining to the company, civil litigation, or pursuing a criminal case—are not a prevention strategy.

As the commissioners who chaired the task force put it in their report, sexual harassment has been a persistent problem. "With legal liability long ago established, with reputational harm from harassment well known, with an entire cottage industry of workplace compliance and training adopted and encouraged for thirty years, why does so much harassment persist and take place in so many of our workplaces?" the report asks.[2] "And, most important of all, what can be done to prevent it?"

Fitzgerald was one of more than a dozen experts called to explain what their work had taught them about sexual harassment and what the research suggests will help eliminate it. "One of the great ideas to come out of that is that we've got to quit putting all responsibility on the complainant to 'handle' the situation," Fitzgerald says.

Specifically, the task force proposed borrowing ideas from bystander intervention trainings, which have been shown to be effective at addressing sexual assault on college campuses. Programs like Green Dot, a program founded in 2009 by Dorothy Edwards, the founding director of the University of Kentucky Violence Intervention and Prevention Center, have already been used widely at universities, in the military, and at a variety of workplaces. Dubbed a "promising practice" by the Centers for Disease Control and

Prevention, Green Dot teaches bystanders and witnesses to harness the power of "peer influence" to disrupt a risky interaction.

The approach is based on the idea that small actions—even subtle interventions—can deter violence, and it ultimately seeks to move people from apathy to actively demonstrating intolerance for violence through even the smallest actions. As Edwards explained to the commission, the name of her organization comes from a simple metaphor: A map of a community awash with small red dots, which symbolize a harmful or violent choice or behavior. "We then suggest dropping a single green dot in the middle of the red dots," Edwards told the commission. "A green dot is a small, single choice that someone makes that reduces the likelihood that the next red dot gets onto the map. . . . The goal is straightforward: When green dots begin to outnumber and displace the red dots, violence is reduced."

Fitzgerald says bystander interventions like the Green Dot model can potentially reshape the culture of an organization or a community into one that doesn't tolerate sexual harassment and violence. "A great deal of harassment is really quite public," Fitzgerald says. "And if you can get other people, allies—really other men—to intervene in some of this, that is one possible way to address this."

The training that took place at Pacific Tomato stands out for its attempts to change organizational culture, but it is also notable because the training is just one piece in a larger effort to create fair and safe working conditions for farmworkers through the Fair Food Program.

The Fair Food Program emerged out of a project of the Coalition of Immokalee Workers that sought to ensure fair and humane working conditions. Since its inception in 2011, the program has been explicit about its goal of reducing sexual harassment and assault in the fields.

The program has attracted attention and praise from the United

Nations and former president Jimmy Carter because it has found a unique way to insist that workers' rights are respected. It leverages consumer power to hold farms responsible for their labor practices while financially incentivizing growers to participate. The program began with a focus on tomato workers in part because Florida, where the Coalition of Immokalee Workers is based, produces a significant percentage of the country's tomatoes. The program has since been expanded to operations in Georgia, North Carolina, South Carolina, Virginia, Maryland, and New Jersey, and to pepper and strawberry crops in Florida.

Through the infrastructure of the Fair Food Program, consumers have a role in demanding that retailers like Whole Foods Market or Taco Bell buy their Florida tomatoes only from farms that participate in the program. These buyers must also pledge to pay roughly a penny more per pound of premium tomatoes, which is passed on to the workers, and they are required to purchase produce from farms that follow the Fair Food code of conduct related to worker conditions.

There's built-in accountability through annual audits and an opportunity to surface complaints through various avenues, such as a confidential complaint line and education sessions. These mechanisms have helped the program address everything from wage problems to sexual assault in the fields.

The audits are an especially novel and effective part of the program. During these site visits—some of which are announced and some of which are not—a team of inspectors meets with upper management to discuss expectations and to make sure the farm is complying with the code of conduct. The team also looks for evidence that the farm has made gains on any lapses observed from previous audits.

Most important, inspectors do a "reality check" with the workers, says Safer Espinoza, the director of the Fair Food Standards Council, which oversees the farm audits. At least half of the front-line supervisors and workers are interviewed to make sure that policies are being followed. Talking directly to a large sample of workers gives the organization a more accurate picture of what is actually happening out in the fields, she says.

To reach the workers, inspectors go where the workers are. They walk alongside tomato pickers in the rows during harvest. They ride the bus with workers from field to field. They visit farmworker housing. Some conversations span five minutes, while others run more than an hour.

During the interviews, workers are asked a host of questions aimed at assessing whether the farm is following the code of conduct. Were they hired directly by the farm as opposed to a third-party farm-labor contractor? What kind of training have they received? What did they think about it?

Inspectors also address the tricky subject of sexual harassment and assault. They ask workers if they are aware of both the program's zero-tolerance policy for sexual harassment and the farm's individual policy. They check into whether the workers have been sexually harassed themselves or if they have witnessed any problems. If the worker describes specific incidents, the inspectors are required to forward the information to the grower.

Sexual harassment and assault is not an easy subject to broach, but the inspectors have refined their approach over the years. In the beginning, they fired off questions in a painfully straightforward way. "People would clam up and not say anything," Safer Espinoza recalls. Now they ask, How is the work environment here for women? How is it for people of different sexual orientations? Or they might ask, Would you be comfortable with your mother or sister working here?

Workers find it easier to confide in the inspectors because the Fair Food Program has a track record of helping workers resolve problems. Calls to the Fair Food Program's twenty-four-hour complaint hotline—where workers can call in confidentially with any kind of job-related problem—are taken by the same inspectors who visit them in the fields during an audit.

Angel García, the human resources manager from Pacific Tomato, says that the Fair Food Program creates an infrastructure that helps growers get a feel for the concerns and complaints of their workers. "There are farmers with good hearts but they are not in the fields and they don't know what is happening in their fields," he says. "Through the audit system, we take the pulse of the operation. We are not a perfect operation but we have a third-party entity and if they find something, we will fix it."

The audits are not just an empty exercise. If sexual harassment is found on a farm, the consequences are swift and serious. For example, if physical sexual harassment by a supervisor is reported, the farm is required to fire that supervisor. If it doesn't, the farm will be suspended from the program and no longer able to sell to the dozen-plus participating buyers, including McDonald's and Walmart.

"I'm amazed how much compliance the ability to sell their product means," Safer Espinoza says. "When you can't make your sales because workers are abused, that is a real issue for the company, and it highly incentivizes compliance."

In the half-dozen years since its founding, the program has made noticeable differences in the fields where it operates, including an improved working environment for female farmworkers. The Fair Food Standards Council's 2015 annual report says that the response to sexual harassment and assault has improved on the farms where they have a presence. In 2012 and 2013, three longtime supervisors were fired for sexual harassment following an audit, which made them ineligible for reemployment for two years among all of the Fair Food growers. In the 2014 and 2015 seasons, the audits did not turn up any cases of violence or sexual assault by supervisors. The program has helped worker advocates "move from prosecution to prevention with regard to sexual violence in the fields," the report says.[3]

Safer Espinoza is confident that Fair Food Program farms reduce sexual violence thanks to the worker rights training, the complaint hotline, and the thorough auditing. "I'd say we have the best chance of knowing about these problems that anyone has ever had in this population," she says. "If there were rampant sexual assault, we'd hear about it through any combination of factors."

She points to the hotline, which has helped the program resolve more than 1,700 worker complaints of all kinds. "The hotline has slowed in terms of seriousness but not in terms of the volume of calls," she says. "We see it as a mechanism for resolving problems,"

It is within this larger context that the sexual harassment and domestic violence training at Pacific Tomato in the spring of 2016 had meaning, says Marley Moynahan of the Coalition of Immokalee Workers, who served as a trainer that day. "If you dropped this training into a farm outside of the Fair Food Program, the workers would connect with what is happening, but the reality is that they would never exercise their rights," she says. "The training is only powerful so far as it translates into reality and a safe place to talk about it."

That the Fair Food Program considers reducing sexual harassment part of ensuring a safe and healthy workplace is a simple but crucial recasting of the problem. It may seem subtle, a matter of semantics, but by defining rape—in the fields, on the janitorial night shift, or in a home that is a caregiver's workplace—as a health and safety issue, it becomes possible to conceive of it as something preventable.

Immigrant women workers whose jobs place them in physical isolation and who are vulnerable to sexual abuse precisely because they face financial, social, and practical barriers to reporting it are at a unique risk for exploitation. Because the dynamics that facilitate the abuse can be reasonably anticipated, it is possible to address them directly. For example, janitorial companies could shift to daytime work hours or assign cleaners to work in pairs. Female farmworkers could work in all-women crews. Domestic workers could wear panic buttons to reach law enforcement if they find themselves attacked and mistreated—as hotel cleaners already do in some parts of the country.

The current focus on helping workers seek recourse means that vulnerable workers are getting assistance only *after* the sexual violence has happened. The women featured in this book who recount being raped or assaulted—Georgina Hernández, who cleaned a Los Angeles hotel lobby; the female farmworkers who labored in the orchards of the Yakima Valley; and June Barrett, who took care of the most personal needs of an elderly man in Miami—certainly would have benefited from an effort to *prevent* on-the-job sexual harassment.

Attempts to reframe extreme sexual harassment as a health and safety issue are gaining traction. In the Yakima Valley of Eastern Washington, Victoria Breckwich Vásquez, a nursing and health studies professor at the University of Washington–Bothell, is bringing together researchers, growers, health clinicians, worker rights advocates, and farmworkers to take steps toward sexual harassment prevention.

Her work is a mainstay of the university's Pacific Northwest Agricultural Safety and Health Center, whose aim is to create safe working conditions for farmworkers. In the past, it has focused on issues like pesticides and heat illness. In recent years, it has turned its attention to sexual harassment and assault in the region's fields and orchards.

"We've been hearing for years that this is an issue that plagues the workplace for agricultural workers," Breckwich Vásquez says, "and no one thought of it as an occupational health issue. We take it for granted that work is one of the safest places to go."

Breckwich Vásquez has focused on reaching the farmworkers in the Yakima Valley with information on how to identify and report sexual harassment so that problems can be addressed before they escalate to extreme levels. She has created a Spanish-language radio drama on the topic, and growers in the area are distributing wallet-size cards that her organization designed with information on how to make complaints about sexual harassment. She is also developing a training video that will draw directly from the experiences of farmworkers—a project that echoes the efforts of the Fair Food Program and its partners—with an evaluation component that will look at whether the training has achieved the desired impact.

Rethinking sexual harassment as a problem that can be tackled through workplace health and safety regulations is a seemingly subtle shift that could have significant impacts. By looking at the issue through the lens of health and safety, Breckwich Vásquez says, she and others pushing for this change are demanding an answer to a fundamental question: "If you don't have security at work, how are you supposed to support your family?"

It's a paradigm shift that has already happened in other countries, like Canada. In Ontario, the province's department of labor sets clear standards and guidelines on how to address workplace sexual coercion. In the United States, though, the concept faces obstacles to wider adoption. Currently, there is no U.S. federal regulation that specifically lays out what is required of employers when it comes to workplace violence prevention in general.[4]

However, under the Occupational Safety and Health Act, an employer must provide a job and workplace "free from recognized hazards that are causing or are likely to cause death or serious physical harm to his employees"—including sexual assault or rape. This responsibility is known as the "general duty clause" of the act.

How to fulfill this responsibility has been the subject of debate and disagreement, because the U.S. Occupational Safety and Health Administration (OSHA) has never issued so-called workplace violence standards, which would spell things out clearly for employers and workers. Instead, OSHA has created voluntary guidelines for employers that are viewed as best practices. OSHA recommends, for instance, that companies draft a written violence prevention plan.

Under the general duty clause, employers are not expected to stop every random act of violence that happens at work. OSHA is, however, empowered to issue a citation and levy a fine against a company if a worker is injured in an act of violence that could have been prevented and reasonably anticipated.

OSHA has focused much of its workplace violence prevention energy on health care workers, late-night retail employees, and taxi drivers. Extreme sexual harassment, such as assault and rape, have not historically been the province of OSHA, although in 2016 there were signs that the agency was beginning to place a greater emphasis on them.

That year, OSHA took its first workplace sexual violence case. A Pennsylvania pediatric nurse reported that she had been sexually assaulted by the father of the child she cared for. OSHA believed that the in-home health care company, Epic Health Services, could have protected its workers from sexual assault if it had offered a system to report and address the attacks. Epic had received complaints from other nurses about physical and sexual assaults from the same man, but it had not taken action to protect employees from his attacks.

The company was fined $98,000, and it received citations for "willful violation" of workplace violence and for failure to report injuries properly to OSHA. "Epic Health Services failed to protect its employees from life-threatening hazards of workplace violence and failed to provide an effective workplace violence prevention program," Richard Mendelson, the OSHA regional administrator in Philadelphia, said in a statement. "No worker should ever have to sacrifice their physical well-being to earn a paycheck."

Since health care and social service workers consistently face the highest rates of job-based violence in the private sector, OSHA also took a significant and laudable step by initiating the development of workplace violence standards for the health care industry in 2016. The process will be lengthy, but if it succeeds in establishing these standards, OSHA can clarify what employers are required to do to prevent violence at work and articulate the kinds of protections workers should expect.

The effort may sound like little more than an exercise in bureaucracy, but the move would create new assurances that workers would be protected from harm. For unions and worker advocacy groups like Worksafe, a California-based worker health and safety advocacy organization, the hope is that the future adoption of standards in one industry will eventually lead to standards for all workers—including farmworkers, janitors, and domestic workers.

It is safe to assume that the creation of the country's first set of national workplace violence standards is a nonstarter under President Donald Trump, who favors reducing regulations on businesses. Under his presidency, OSHA will likely focus less on policing violations and more on helping companies follow existing rules. Congress, with the president's backing, has also scaled back worker safety regulations implemented during the Obama administration.

Efforts to prevent sexual violence in the workplace are more likely to happen state by state. New York State already has workplace violence standards that apply to public employees.[5] Washington State has implemented regulations for people working in health care facilities, psychiatric hospitals, and late-night retail outlets, such as convenience stores.[6] And in 2016, following more than two years of advocacy, California created new rules for health care employers that are considered some of the toughest in the nation.[7]

The push for a workplace violence standard in California began in 2010, when two San Francisco Bay Area health care workers were killed on the job within a week. First, a Napa State Hospital employee named Donna Gross was strangled to death by a psychiatric patient. Days later, Cynthia Palomata, a nurse working at a jail in the San Francisco Bay Area, was hit on the head with a lamp so brutally by an inmate that she fell into a coma. She was removed from life support three days later.

These incidents galvanized the state's health care workers and brought wider public attention to an ongoing problem. To eliminate some of the risks of the job, the unions representing nurses—the California Nurses Association/National Nurses Organizing Committee and the Service Employees International Union—both began pushing for legislation that would require some hospitals to create workplace violence prevention plans. After one failed legislative attempt, the bill passed in the fall of 2014.

Months before that bill passed, the unions sought another route to improving job safety for health care workers. Each union petitioned the state's department of labor for a workplace violence standard to demand that employers become more proactive about reducing violence in their industry. "We recognize that you cannot eliminate all violence in the workplace but you can make an honest attempt to eliminate it as much as possible," says Katherine Hughes, a registered nurse and the executive director of the Service Employees International Union Nurse Alliance of California.

Given the overlap between the petitions and the state law that the union had fought for, the state's Occupational Health and Safety Standards Board began exploring a workplace violence standard for health care workers that could incorporate the requirements of the law. But first, the standards board had to overcome internal skepticism about the issue. At the first hearing, Hughes remembers a board member telling the crowd that workplace violence in nursing "isn't a big problem" and that it's better tackled by law enforcement after the fact.

The board became more committed to the issue after health care workers began to offer testimony at public hearings about workplace violence. Two women in Southern California had been stabbed in separate hospitals in the same weekend. One nurse had been kicked in the head by a patient and had suffered a concussion. A female nurse was raped in a medicine closet. "After hearing these stories and realizing what a problem it was on a human level, they realized they could do something about it," Hughes says of the board.

The board also had questions about how employers could be expected to prevent what might seem like random acts of violence, which led to discussions about the foreseeable nature of the violence that health care workers face. "Most violent incidents come with some of kind of warning," Hughes says. "They don't go from zero to sixty in a breath."

The scenarios and infrastructure that facilitate violence is where intervention can begin, Hughes says. Work areas can be redesigned. Workers can be taught de-escalation techniques and given self-defense training.

In the spring of 2017, some of the workplace violence standards for California health care workers began to go into effect. Going forward, California businesses and organizations that employ certain kinds of health care workers are required to conduct violence risk assessments and then create prevention plans. These plans require the input of workers, under the logic that they are the ones most aware of the potential hazards of their jobs.

Under this new system, health care workers are also able to make complaints if they feel that a hospital or health care facility is not following its prevention plan. Employers are prohibited from retaliating against anyone who raises an issue, and they are required to evaluate the prevention plan each year in conjunction with front-line workers.

Plans to expand these protections to all California workers are already in the works, with a state committee analyzing the feasibility of creating a workplace violence standard for a wide range of jobs and industries. As this process moves forward, advocates like Nicole Márquez of Worksafe are working to ensure that the experiences of low-wage immigrant workers will be specifically considered. In particular, Márquez says, her organization will point to the needs of women working in the janitorial, hotel housekeeping, and agricultural industries, whose workers are particularly vulnerable. Of the organization's goals, Márquez says simply, "Violence should not be part of the job."

Employers, however, continue to have concerns about the standard. In some industries, like construction, employers say that workplace violence is not a problem. Others have expressed concern that the California requirements are overbroad and will subject them to undue liability. In an online editorial, two lawyers from BakerHostetler, a firm that represents employers, described California's workplace violence standards for health care workers as "broad, unclear obligations on health care employers who now must design a program to protect employees from seemingly unpredictable acts of violence perpetrated by virtually anyone on the premises."

On one point, however, both advocates and opponents of the new standards are in agreement: it won't be long before other states—and maybe one day, the federal government—take a similar approach to workplace violence prevention. "California has set an extreme tone in establishing such a far-reaching workplace safety standard, and federal and other state OSHAs will look to these standards when addressing this issue," the BakerHostetler lawyers wrote in their editorial.

For nurse advocate Bonnie Castillo, the director of health and safety for the California Nurses Association/National Nurses United, widespread adoption of the workplace violence standards is exactly the point. "We know that these protections are necessary across America," Castillo said in a statement, "and that's why it's so important that California can now serve as a model for the nation."

7

¡Sí Se Pudo! Yes We Did!

The circumstances that led to Georgina Hernández being raped while cleaning a Los Angeles hotel began decades before she took a job as a janitor.

Hernández had been born and raised in a small village in Puebla, a state in south-central Mexico, and she was the oldest of nine siblings. When she was ten, their father abandoned the family, and she was left to take care of her siblings while her mother worked. His departure robbed Hernández of an education, and it thrust the family deeper into poverty, but it was also a relief, because he had been physically abusive of them.

Whatever work her mother cobbled together never seemed to be enough, so Hernández helped her mother finance the family's survival. Their neighbors noticed Hernández's resourcefulness and industry with her younger siblings, and though she was a child herself, they hired her to take care of their kids or clean their houses.

Poverty was compounded by violence. When Hernández was a teenager, a family friend raped her, and she became pregnant. Terminating the pregnancy wasn't an option, so to continue supporting her siblings and provide for the new baby, she took a job at a factory.

Hernández was a diligent and fast worker, and she caught the attention of a man who would become the father of her next five children. He was older, and she liked the way he talked to her in the beginning. "When I met him, I thought he was a good person because he told me I was a very good young lady, that I got ahead, that I was helping my family," Hernández says.

The relationship became a way to escape her mother's house, which always seemed heavy with hunger and uncontrolled emotions. She moved in with him when her baby was about a year old, and within a couple of years, she was pregnant with twin boys. She had always fantasized about having her own home and raising a big family, and it felt like the start of her dream coming true.

Within a few years, she was pregnant again with another boy. Then over the course of another half-dozen years, she had two more children, first a girl and then a boy. Even with so many young children to tend to, Hernández continued to do what she had become expert in: working and earning money. She took ironing and sewing jobs, working at night when the kids were sleeping.

She also volunteered for a political party, and in exchange, it gave her the cement, sand, and gravel to build an addition to the house. Her long-held dream was slowly becoming a reality. "My dream was to have my own home, to have a home for my children," she says, "I made that dream come true. I had a very pretty home. My house was what I'd never had before. And I had my children, and I felt very happy. But I worked too hard."

Another problem was her children's father, who traveled between the United States and Mexico for work, and who was growing resentful of the number of kids he had to support. She dreaded his return home. Behind his charm and flattery was an unsteady temper. When he got angry, he berated Hernández, telling her that she was ignorant and a disgrace. Or he took out his rage on her physically, just as her father had on her and her mother. Hernández learned to absorb the violence. She tried to tolerate it through sheer resolve because, with six kids, she didn't see a clear way out, and she was tethered to the house and the dream it represented.

"There were times I couldn't stand it, and I'd tell myself, 'If I leave, I'm going to leave all this, which has cost me so much,'" she says. "But there came a day that I couldn't . . . I couldn't do it anymore, couldn't bear so much. And I decided to leave him."

That is when he told her he had put the deed of the house—the one that she had put so much into building and improving—in his parents' name only. "There was nothing left to fight for," she says.

After fifteen years together, she left. The only place to go was her mother's house, which was already crowded with a handful of her brothers and sisters. Now with Hernández and her kids, there would be seven more, all of them in one room.

Hernández did her best to plod forward, though there came a moment when the daily fight overcame her tenacity, and her resourcefulness and grit didn't provide a way forward. She had lost her house. All of the work that she did never added up to enough food to feed her kids or send them to school. "I'd look at my children and look at how poor I was," she says. "I didn't know what to feed them. That was when I thought to myself, *I no longer have anything in my life, my life is worthless.*"

She left her mother's house and began to walk one afternoon, dazed and devastated. She ended up at the intersection of a busy road. Without looking, she stepped into the traffic and began to walk. A few steps later, she was hit by a truck.

"It wasn't an accident," she says. "I had intended to kill myself."

Hernández ended up in the hospital for three weeks. During her recovery, she overheard the nurses speculating that she had been in an accident because she was an alcoholic. As broken as she was, it made her indignant. "How is it that this is what people think of me, that this is who I am?" she thought. "They say that because they don't know what I've been through."

Hernández settled on a Hail Mary: she would support her children by going to the United States to find work. Her cousin and brother were already planning to go. They had a coyote lined up to guide them through the desert and across the Mexico-California border. She would have to find $5,000 to travel with them.

Her mother hated the idea, and her oldest children were vocal in their opposition. Hernández did not truly want to go either—her youngest child was only six months old at the time—but her children had known only a pattern of poverty and hunger, and her inability to provide for them was even more devastating than the idea of leaving them behind.

Three weeks after leaving the hospital, she was in the desert with more than a dozen people, including her cousin and her fourteen-year-old brother. They walked at night, and the two sweatshirts Hernández wore did not ward off the cold. Her legs were weak from the hospitalization and she still wore a cervical collar around her neck.

There was only a short distance left to go when someone yelled out, "¡La migra!" With the medical collar on, Hernández couldn't turn her head, so she ran straight ahead. Out of the corner of her eye, she watched as immigration agents took her brother and put him into the back of a truck. She thought about giving herself up, too, but then she thought of her children. "I said, God, I have a purpose and I don't want to go back," Hernández says.

She hid under a tree, and though the border patrol swept the area, they never passed their lights down low, where she was crouching. Once they had passed, she calmed herself by drinking a little water and washing her face from a small trickle of water that she found on the ground. She kept still, certain that the group would come looking for her. No one did. She had to keep walking. *If I'm not dead yet, I'm not going to die*, she said to herself. *I'm going to cross.* "And that was how I was lost for a whole night in the desert by myself," she says.

In time, she heard a noise in the brush. The coyote had given them a code if they came across other people but were not sure if they were friendly or not. One person would say "one, two" and the correct response was "one, two."

"Uno, dos," Hernández said, tentatively.

"Uno, dos," came the reply from the bushes.

They both emerged from the brush, and in a stroke of serendipity, the other person was her cousin. Hernández tearfully told him that her brother had been dragged off by *la migra*. Her cousin tried to console her, and she came to accept that he was right when he said that they had to just keep on moving. Physically, though, she didn't think she do it. Her cousin asked the coyote to give her a pill to numb the pain.

By the end of the journey, Hernández's feet were torn up and blistered. Her calves were swollen. To get to the van that would take them to Los Angeles, they had to jump from a tall fence and Hernández was afraid she'd break her legs. But she made it. Of the fifteen people who had started with them, there were now only four in the van headed north to the city.

They were taken to a safe house for the night until her sister, who had made the trek to Los Angeles years before, came to pick her up. Hernández slept a few hours, and the next day, her feet and legs still aching, she went to look for work in Los Angeles's garment district. Her sister tried to encourage her to rest for a few days because Hernández was clearly dehydrated and sickly. Hernández told her sister she had no choice. "I left my children without money," she said.

The first garment factory turned her away because she didn't have her own sewing plates, spindle, or scissors. At factory after factory, it was the same. There was no work if she didn't bring her own materials. It was a catch-22: Hernández didn't have any money to buy the equipment, but she couldn't get a job without it. After visiting nearly a half-dozen factories, she caught a break when she met a man outside of a factory that produced clothes for a fancy name brand. He said he would lend her some sewing plates for the day. If she got the job, he would expect payment.

Inside, Hernández was given a test. The supervisor gave her a sample blouse and told her to have one finished by the middle of the day. Hernández nearly scoffed. She completed it in three hours. They hired her on the spot and asked her to stay and finish out the day.

She worked at the garment factory for a year. It was a good job that paid decently because Hernández sewed quickly. She remembers one particularly good week when she earned $700 after making hundreds of pairs of pants. But the supervisor made the job hard to take. She could almost put up with the his insults and yelling— that they looked like elephants, that they ate too much, that they used too much toilet paper in the bathroom. What she hated most about the job was that her supervisor scared her. Rumors circulated that he had a Jacuzzi in his office, where he would demand sex from female workers whom he called in to meet with him.

He had already summoned Hernández to his office a few times, but she had never gone, because she knew what showing up might mean. But she had been doing good work and she needed a raise. She was sending money back to her kids and her mother every two weeks. Her remittances plus the rent she paid for a single room in a crowded Los Angeles apartment never left her enough to survive on. Sometimes she was late with her rent, and sometimes she didn't have enough money to eat. She took the risk and went to the supervisor's office to ask for more money.

When she got to his office, he told her to take a seat. She explained that she needed a raise, and the supervisor told her that coincidentally, the factory had landed a new client, and he was looking for someone to supervise the line. It was a promotion with a raise, but before she could agree to it, he dropped a pair of pants on the floor next to him and said, "Pick it up."

Hernández asked him why he wanted her to pick them up, since she was seated on the other side of the desk. "Well, I'm paying you to pick it up," he replied. Hernández walked over and bent down to pick up the pants. Her supervisor turned toward her with his zipper undone.

She grabbed the pants and handed them to him before running out of the office. Flustered, she told a co-worker that she couldn't work there anymore because the supervisor scared her. "This is not good what he is doing," Hernández said.

The co-worker encouraged her to take it in stride, because the supervisor was rich and he would pay her well if Hernández did what she was told. After all, her co-worker had said, all he asked you to do was pick up a pair of pants.

Hernández quit. Soon after, she got her job as a janitor on the night shift.

When Georgina Hernández was harassed and then raped by her supervisor at the hotel that she cleaned, she was one in a legion of janitors who worked for a small cleaning company with no real physical or business infrastructure. More than 60 percent of janitors work for similar enterprises—hard-to-find businesses that have fewer than four employees and sign contracts to clean buildings spread throughout a city or region.[1] The cleaning company's workers are then dispatched to these far-flung spaces alone or in small groups, usually at night. An on-site supervisor may be the only representative of the company that they ever interact with, a situation that gives the supervisor a significant amount of power to wield.

As an undocumented single mother working for a little-noticed operation in a notoriously opaque industry, Hernández was an obvious target for an unscrupulous supervisor. By most expectations, her rape claims were transgressions that should have remained hidden. As a newcomer, she didn't know what her rights were or whom she could trust to ask for help. And because her job is deliberately made invisible, it was difficult for worker advocates to reach her. Hernández found help only because of her improbable encounter with Vicky Márquez of the Maintenance Cooperation Trust Fund during one of organization's nighttime undercover outreach operations. Márquez and the organization became a lifeline to Hernández, helping her resolve problems with her paycheck, and supporting her through the aftermath of the sexual attacks.

In other low-wage industries where female immigrants tend to flock, worker-led organizations have similarly stepped in when there are few safety nets for women abused at work. For servers and bartenders, there's the Restaurant Opportunities Center United, which was started in New York City and now has nine local affiliates throughout the country. In domestic work, there are organizations that collaborate with the National Domestic Workers Alliance, such as the Brazilian Workers Center in Massachusetts or the Southwest Workers Union in Texas. For California farmworkers, Líderes Campesinas and Campesinas Unidas have, for decades, hosted community events to educate workers about sexual harassment, and held meetings in houses and backyards so that women can discuss health and safety issues, like sexual abuse. This type of support is especially important for workers so determined to keep their jobs that they are not likely to report a problem. "When they know they can have some type of security, some kind of protection, then they'll come forth," says Dolores Huerta, the farmworker organizer who co-founded the United Farm Workers in 1962. "But it takes a lot. It takes a lot."

Worker advocates say that if Georgina Hernández had been part of a labor union, things might have been different. At the very least, she would have had a more direct path to finding help. But unions have had their own struggles with addressing on-the-job sexual harassment and assault, and it's not an issue on which organized labor has historically led the way.

For the bulk of the last century, labor unions focused on

improving the wages, hours, and working conditions of male workers in industrial jobs.[2] Although the earliest unions in the United
States, such as the Knights of Labor and the Industrial Workers
of the World, were inclusive of women, minorities, and unskilled
workers, the dominant unions at the dawn of the twentieth century
were founded and led by men in the craft trades.[3] Marion G. Crain,
a law professor, and Ken Matheny, a federal government attorney,
have co-authored law journal articles about organized labor, and
they observed that these male-dominated unions historically focused on job protection and workplace organizing in skilled professions that resulted in the exclusion of minorities and women, or
at the very least made it difficult for these groups to meaningfully
participate. Under this model of organizing, they wrote, "White
male shop floor culture was the foundation of solidarity."[4]

The experiences and issues important to female workers, such as
sexual harassment, were not prioritized by the unions where men
made up the bulk of the rank and file, the organizers, the bargaining committee members, and the leaders. As a result, by the middle of the twentieth century, women and minorities began turning
to the government to address the problem as a form of workplace
discrimination.[5]

In recent decades, female participation and leadership in unions
has increased, but like every type of organization, unions have negotiated internal struggles around racism and sexism with varying
degrees of progress. "The labor movement is a microcosm of society," says KC Wagner, director of workplace issues at Cornell University's Industry and Labor Relations School. Constituency groups
of unions have sought to bring together diverse workers to address
labor issues across industries and workplaces. The Coalition of
Labor Union Women, for example, has been crucial in advancing
discussion and action on issues that affect female workers, such as
sexual harassment.

Wagner has been working with unions for more than thirty

years to incorporate the experiences of women workers into the organized labor agenda. Before that, she was the counseling director of the Working Women's Institute, an organization founded in 1975 by a sexual harassment victim, and one of the country's first community-based organizations to focus on the issue. In those roles, Wagner has seen the incremental change in perception and awareness around sexual violence at work. At the Working Women's Institute in the early 1980s, Wagner came to see how deeply misunderstood the problem was. At the time, the prevailing notion in many workplaces was that sexual harassment was the natural order of things, a problematic idea accompanied by the faulty yet enduring assumption that victims would naturally report or confront the perpetrators.

The thinking within male-dominated unions was no different. Workplace sexual harassment and assault were either misunderstood or simply not on the radar of the men who made up the bulk of the union membership and leadership. Unions were forced, however, to take a closer look at the subject in 1980, when the U.S. Equal Employment Opportunity Commission issued its first guidelines on sexual harassment. Simultaneously, an emerging docket of sexual harassment lawsuits began to drive home the point that there were consequences for workers who harass and penalties for companies that allow it to happen. "That really signaled a wave in unions addressing it because the law had identified it as a problem," Wagner says. "Prior to that, people thought that this was just what happened between men and women."

Beginning in the 1970s, as more women entered the workforce, organizations focused on women's equality in jobs and education, such as 9to5, Equal Rights Advocates, and the Family Violence Prevention Fund (now known as Futures Without Violence) pushed employers and unions to take greater responsibility for addressing sexual harassment. The first unions to directly take on the issue tended to have a larger number of women on their membership rolls, such as the United Auto Workers, which had seen an influx of women workers—a trend embodied by the cultural icon Rosie the Riveter—during World War II.

As with many organizations, labor union attention to sexual harassment increased after Anita Hill testified at Clarence Thomas's confirmation hearing. A year later, in 1992, the American Federation of State, County and Municipal Employees, the country's largest union for public service employees, adopted a resolution explicitly condemning sexual harassment. The union represents the job sector where female union membership has been the largest.[6]

The growth in female union leadership has also prompted greater attention to issues like sexual harassment within organized labor itself. Dolores Huerta says that at various points during her work with the United Farm Workers in the 1960s and 1970s, she had to push the men she worked with to become more aware of the offhand sexist comments they were making. "That's why it's so important to have women involved," Huerta says. "The best way to curb this type of macho sexist culture is to make sure that women are involved."

At Cornell's Industrial Labor Relations School, KC Wagner has spent the past few decades training unions about sexual and gendered violence in the workplace. For some unions and some members, the relevance of these issues has not always been clear, so she has developed strategies to help them see the connections between sexual violence and the values that unions hold dear. "If you see it as a structural issue, as a violation of rights, then you can create the link to how this connects to workplace rights and worker rights," Wagner says.

She has reminded unions and their members that they all share core values related to social justice, mutual aid, and solidarity, and she asserts that combating sexual violence at work speaks directly to that. If sexual harassment or violence is dismissed by a union as a private matter, she helps them see that it undermines worker productivity and efficiency. She has told unions that, just as they emphasize protective gear and safety protocols, they should work to prevent sexual violence, which is a workplace safety issue too.

Skepticism among some unions and their members has not completely fallen away. During a recent training on sexual violence and domestic violence, she was told that she was just being "politically correct." She assured the audience that there was more to it than hewing to a party line. In addition to shared values of dignity and respect in the workplace, she told the group, "This is about the law, about efficiency and productivity, and it's about conflict resolution."

These days, there is greater awareness of sexual harassment within unions—and throughout society as a whole—than when Wagner first began this work three decades ago. Though it remains a marginalized issue, it has increasingly become an accepted issue for union advocacy. These days, sexual harassment prevention and protection is often incorporated into contracts during negotiations. It is not uncommon for union committees on workplace safety or women's issues to sponsor sexual harassment training for their members. This is the case among the country's largest unions. The Service Employees International Union provides training to its locals, and the American Federation of Labor–Congress of Industrial Organizations (AFL-CIO) advanced an "Economic Agenda for Working Women and Our Families" in 2016 that specifically called for ending workplace violence and harassment. Wagner is involved in developing both a training program that the AFL-CIO will offer to its affiliates and a survey of workers on gender-based violence. Taken together, these efforts are a move to shift the cultural norms of a worksite or industry so that sexual harassment is not tolerated, a tactic that researchers like Louise Fitzgerald, John Pryor, and others have found can minimize the problem. "There are so many levels, looking at how unions are structured, that they can make sexual harassment prevention part of the lifeblood of the union," Wagner says.

Of course, the presence of unions alone doesn't eliminate sexual harassment or assault at work. These cases can be especially complicated for unions because they have a duty to provide "fair representation" to every union member, which means they might find themselves representing both the accuser and the accused in the sexual harassment claims against the employer. "It's not that unions condone the behavior, but they do need to make sure there is due process," Wagner says.

The tensions for unions that come from representing both the accuser and the accused were highlighted in a case involving a San Francisco cleaner named María Bojórquez, who had taken a cleaning job in 2004. She worked for one of the country's largest cleaning companies, ABM Industries, which is unionized in many cities. It has dealt with its share of sexual harassment complaints, and the company says that it is a target for sexual harassment lawsuits precisely because it is a large corporation with deep pockets. And unlike underground operations or the tiny businesses that make up the bulk of the janitorial industry, ABM says it is a professionally run corporation with a human resources department that offers workers sexual harassment training and a process for lodging complaints. "ABM is committed to fostering a professional and safe work environment for all of our employees," a representative of the company said in a statement.[7] "We have implemented comprehensive state of the art policies and procedures to prevent harassment. These are provided to employees beginning when they are hired and again on a continuing basis."

Even so, among large companies, ABM has seen a number of sexual harassment lawsuits involving extreme claims. It is among a small group of more than two dozen American companies that have been sued by the U.S. Equal Employment Opportunity Commission multiple times for sexual harassment. Two of those cases against ABM involved allegations of on-the-job rape.

Bojórquez brought another sexual harassment claim against

the company in 2010. It, too, made a charge of workplace rape. Bojórquez had been assigned to clean law offices in San Francisco's iconic Ferry Building. Soon after she started the job, her boss began making her uncomfortable when he used sexual language around her and looked for excuses to touch her buttocks and breasts when he came by to monitor her work. About six weeks into the job, the supervisor called Bojórquez into an office and told her to pick up tiny pieces of paper that had fallen on the floor. When she went to begin the task, she says, he tripped her and raped her where she fell.

Bojórquez was let go, and she eventually filed a sexual harassment lawsuit against ABM with the help of Equal Rights Advocates, a women's rights and legal advocacy organization. Though sexual harassment cases rarely go to trial, her case went before a jury two years later. It found in Bojórquez's favor. ABM appealed the verdict, and the case was settled in 2015. In settling, the company denied liability but agreed to make a payout to Bojórquez and to implement an outside review process for rape and attempted rape claims. The accused foreman also denied the allegations at trial.

Bojórquez's David-and-Goliath case—a single janitor winning a jury trial against a multibillion-dollar company—brought sustained attention to the problem, changes at the company, and some justice for Bojórquez. At the same time, unionization protected the accused foreman's job. After the company's internal investigation was completed—the case was deemed "inconclusive" because ABM could not find corroborating evidence of Bojórquez's claims—he filed a union grievance against ABM for moving him from his preferred worksite. The union helped him negotiate an agreement that led to a permanent move to another location with the same pay, benefits, and seniority. During Bojórquez's lawsuit, the union had also filed an affidavit that supported one of the company's legal positions that would help ABM limit its liability for the alleged rape.

Unions operate under the weight of a complex political calculus when handling sexual harassment claims, and many do not have a long tradition of tackling the issue proactively. Sometimes, union officials are themselves the perpetrators. Undeniably, organized labor's influence and reach on the issue is significant. "Unions can be agents of change or agents in maintaining the status quo," says Jennifer Reisch, an attorney with Equal Rights Advocates who represented María Bojórquez. "What cases like María's do is help force organized labor and employers to realize that the status quo is not okay."

In 2016, four years after Bojórquez's case went to trial, the SEIU United Workers West, the janitor's union in California, made a decisive choice to deploy its energy and activism toward abolishing workplace sexual violence. In the process, it became exemplary of what a union can accomplish when it resolves to take the lead.

When Vicky Márquez of the Maintenance Cooperation Trust Fund met Georgina Hernández on a nighttime undercover investigation, she could not have predicted that years later Hernández would launch California's fight against rape on the night shift. At first, Márquez and her co-workers were focused on helping the janitor file a set of wage-and-hour claims with the California Labor Commissioner's Office against the companies that had forced her to clean movie theaters and other entertainment venues without paying her what she was due.

After Hernández was raped and turned to Márquez for help, the organization concentrated on helping the janitor out of crisis. Emboldened by the support of the Maintenance Cooperation Trust Fund, Hernández decided to seek justice through official channels. She filed a police report and a sexual harassment lawsuit against the cleaning company she had worked for and the supervisor who she said had raped her.

In 2014, Hernández received news about both of her cases. In the spring, about three years after she'd filed a wage-and-hour claim with the state, she learned that the government had levied nearly $1.8 million in financial penalties against the companies and their owners. Then, a few months later, the sexual harassment lawsuit was resolved in a confidential settlement. The company did not admit liability in settling the case.[8]

In the process of claiming her rights, Hernández was beginning to see that by making just demands, winning was possible. When the Maintenance Cooperation Trust Fund helped lead an industry-wide effort to battle wage theft by janitorial companies, Hernández joined the fight.

Wage theft is a phenomenon first articulated by Kim Bobo, the founder of Interfaith Worker Justice, which is dedicated to improving pay rates and working conditions, especially for low-wage laborers. Bobo observed that billions of dollars were being stolen from workers when employers failed to pay workers what they were owed, either by demanding off-the-clock labor, not paying for overtime, violating minimum wage laws, misclassifying workers, taking illegal deductions, or simply not paying workers at all.[9]

These were wage scams that Hernández had experienced personally, and they were rampant in her community. A 2014 study by the UCLA Labor Center and others had found that the practice of underpaying low-wage workers was widespread, with dishonest employers stealing more than $26 million a week from Los Angeles workers alone.[10] According to the researchers, this made Southern California the "wage theft capital of the United States."[11]

In February 2015, an anti–wage theft bill backed by the janitors' union and other labor advocates was introduced in the California legislature.[12] It sought to crack down on employers who skirted wage-and-hour laws, and Hernández became a poster child for the cause. She volunteered to go to the state capitol to lobby and testify for its passage. She and her four-year-old daughter became fixtures at rallies in support of the legislation, where she marched alongside her advocates and friends at the Maintenance Cooperation Trust Fund. She became an unofficial spokeswoman of the problem. "No overtime, no break. No lunch. Nada," Hernández told a Los Angeles public radio reporter during the legislative campaign. "When I asked about overtime, the manager said I was crazy."[13] She added that she was working to support her children.

That fall, the wage-theft bill passed, and it fed Hernández's commitment to political activism. She had already won a personal victory by filing her own wage claim, and now she had helped leverage her experiences to help other low-wage workers. Lilia García, executive director of the Maintenance Cooperation Trust Fund, says, "The wage theft work helped her understand and see how people take on problems systematically."

But Hernández wasn't done. At a celebration of the passage of the wage-theft bill thrown by the janitor's union in Los Angeles, Hernández was asked to speak. She started by thanking the politicians in the room who had supported the legislation. Then she stunned the room when she added, "but we still have more work to do; so much more happens than our wages get stolen." Though she could barely choke out the words, she told the audience that when she was a janitor, her supervisor had raped her at work. She said workplace sexual assault needed to be addressed too.

The room fell silent. Hernández's words had given the audience a palpable jolt. Like many people at the event, Alejandra Valles, the secretary-treasurer and chief of staff of SEIU United Workers West, was moved to tears by Hernández's impromptu rallying cry, and Valles vowed to do something about a problem that the union had known about for too long. The issue carried a personal charge for Valles because she, too, was a sexual assault survivor.

For the union leaders, however, this was new territory, and it was not initially clear how they would find their way forward. Valles teamed up with her colleague Sandra Díaz, SEIU United Workers West's political director, to seek out more information about the problem. As a first step, they suggested that the union leadership watch "Rape on the Night Shift," the PBS *Frontline* documentary about workplace assaults in the cleaning industry, at their next executive board meeting. Valles says that for the union leaders in the room, it helped drive home the point that sexual violence for janitorial workers wasn't a rare, isolated phenomenon.

An opportunity for the union to directly address sexual harassment and assault came a few months later. In February 2016, the union prepared for contract negotiations with all unionized janitorial firms, including California's largest janitorial employers, such as ABM. As is standard operating procedure, it sent out a survey asking its members about their workplace priorities, which then informs the bargaining committee's efforts. Following Georgina Hernández's memorable speech, Valles and her colleagues added sexual violence and harassment to the survey to see if it was an issue that resonated with their twenty thousand janitorial members.

About a quarter of janitors in California who work for private companies are unionized, and when the five thousand survey results were tallied a few weeks later, wages and workload were, predictably, the top two priorities for the rank and file.[14] "We tend to fight for things that members can see in their pockets," Valles says.

To the union leadership's amazement and horror, however, sexual violence and harassment ranked as the third most important issue to their membership, the majority of whom are women. Worse, about half of the union's members reported that they had personally experienced sexual violence or harassment. "This was just alarming," Valles says. "As a union that represents predominantly immigrant janitors and seventy percent of them are women, I just said we can't be a janitors' union if we don't do anything about this. We have to take on this issue that is rampant in this industry."

First, some of the rank and file needed convincing. With the survey results tabulated, the union held a general meeting so its members could vote on their priorities for the contract negotiations, including the issues the union would be willing to strike for. About five hundred union members turned up for the Southern California meeting, and when wages and workload were presented as strike priorities, there was no disagreement among the assembly. Things took a turn when a union member named Veronica Laguna informed the group that sexual harassment and violence had come in as the third most important concern to the membership and that it, too, would become a strike priority. As she spoke, a low roar emerged from the audience. Some of the men in the crowd were booing her.

Stunned, Laguna handed the microphone to the union president, David Huerta, who silenced the group by saying that their union couldn't claim to fight for justice for janitors and then turn a blind eye to sexual harassment and assault. "I've been in this industry for twenty years and don't tell me you don't do it and you haven't seen it," he said to the men in the audience. "And now, as your president, I say to you, '*Ya basta.*'" Enough is enough.

Valles says the incident made it clear to the union leadership that they had to overcome the misconception that "women's issues are not worker issues," she says. "There was a macho mentality we were taking on. We came out of there saying, 'How do we engage the men to also be allies?' So it's not just the women who are invested in this."

During contract negotiations, the bargaining committee remained true to the priorities outlined in the membership survey and made demands for improved wages and working conditions, plus a slate of new policies to address sexual violence and harassment on the job.

Now it was the employers' turn to push back against the union's efforts to stop the abuse. "They already considered themselves leaders on wages and benefits and they think they're the good guys, and in many ways, they are," Valles says of the unionized employers. "They were saying that we should focus on the bad guys. But one of them was the biggest culprit. They knew they weren't clean, and we demanded that they lead on this. Our duty as a union is to set standards on working conditions and these [sexual abuse claims] are working conditions."

The union successfully negotiated the inclusion of new contract language that would forbid janitorial supervisors from "dating" their subordinates. The new contract also required janitorial companies to provide information about a free crisis hotline and to offer sexual harassment training to all workers within sixty days of being hired.

Before it could be signed, the union held another meeting so that all of its members could ratify what the bargaining committee had negotiated. A thousand members from Southern California showed up and took seats on folding chairs lined up in the union hall. An overflow crowd listened from the parking lot. When it was time to discuss what the union had won on sexual harassment and assault prevention, Veronica Laguna, the woman who had been booed at the last meeting, returned to the stage. She received a warmer welcome this time. As she told the group about the gains the union had made on sexual harassment, female workers threw their fists in the air in solidarity. The contract with the new sexual harassment provisions was signed in May 2016.

Even as SEIU United Workers West tackled sexual violence in its contract negotiations and made headway among resistant factions of the membership, its leaders were still forced to acknowledge that they were in unchartered territory. "Some people said, 'Well hold on, we're not social workers. We can't take this on. What are we going to do? It's like we're going to become like a rape center or something,'" Valles recalls.

The union has a history of working closely with the Maintenance Cooperation Trust Fund, which has its office in the union's complex just south of downtown Los Angeles. They had already been victorious in their collaborative effort to pass California's new wage-theft legislation. They decided that workplace sexual violence was another issue on which they could work together. Valles and Díaz of the union began having conversations with the Maintenance Cooperation Trust Fund's Lilia García about what could be done to support the next Georgina Hernández who came through the door. García suggested that they reach out to the executive director of the California Coalition Against Sexual Assault. After a lengthy phone conversation with the director, the worker advocates realized that their respective organizations did not need to reinvent themselves at all; they just needed to find a better way to collaborate with organizations like the East Los Angeles Women's Center, which had been working with Spanish-speaking immigrant survivors of sexual violence for decades. The organization is esteemed within the immigrant community of Southern California. In 1976, it had created the country's first twenty-four-hour crisis hotline in Spanish for sexual assault survivors.

The union and the Maintenance Cooperation Trust Fund contacted the center, which was eager to help, but it had never examined the problem in the context of the workplace. Its officers agreed to develop a leadership program specifically for sexually abused workers. The center proposed a *promotora* program to let the janitors' know that sexual harassment and abuse are not acceptable at work and to give them concrete information about how to seek help.

The center has a long history of cultivating *promotoras*, public health advocates who come from the community they seek to reach. *Promotoras* are typically educated on a specific health or social issue and then charged with training others in the community, a peer-to-peer approach used often in Latin America.

The model was popularized in the 1970s by a nonprofit in Mexico that began using this method to provide improved maternal and child health care to impoverished communities in Juárez, on the other side of the border from El Paso, Texas. Prevention and intervention is key to *promotora* programs, which offer critical public health information to groups that institutionalized medical and government programs cannot easily access.

It's a strategy that is now widely used to improve public health in the United States, and it has been especially effective in propagating information among hard-to-reach groups because the information is offered in culturally and linguistically relevant ways. The Centers for Disease Control and Prevention have created materials for *promotora* programs on health issues such as cervical cancer, diabetes, and heart attack prevention.

The approach was already familiar to the union and the Maintenance Cooperation Trust Fund because they had used similar methods to empower and train workers like Georgina Hernández on employment issues like wage theft. Hernández, for example, had been taught how to keep track of her hours and monitor her paychecks to make sure she was paid what she was due, and she had shared the information with her co-workers.

At the first janitor-*promotora* training, which began in March 2016 and ran over the course of six Saturdays, the women learned how to identify sexual harassment and violence at work, as well as what their options are if it happens to them. When they were done, they were asked to reach out and train other female workers in the union and in the community. Given the negative reaction that some of the men had during contract negotiations, the center also created a men's group so that supportive male workers were better equipped to help challenge sexism and harassment at work.

A half-dozen union and non-union cleaners were picked to participate in the inaugural class of *promotoras*. They had been chosen because they had already been unusually outspoken on sexual harassment and assault by filing lawsuits or union grievances. Naturally, Georgina Hernández was among them, and she quickly assumed a quiet but powerful leadership role. During one session, she emboldened other women to share their experiences openly after she worked up the courage to tell the group about how her supervisor had raped her, in the back seat of his car, and twice more in a motel. She described how sunken and stuck she had felt when she learned she was pregnant from one of the assaults. And she said that the women at the Maintenance Cooperation Trust Fund had shown her that she not only had options, but that she could demand justice.

The women in the group followed Hernández's trajectory from resignation to resistance. For the *promotoras* in training, who grappled with longstanding taboos around sex, this was the first opportunity that many of them had to speak openly about sexual harassment and assault. A woman named Marta from San Diego shared a story about her supervisor who had shown her pictures of his genitals on his phone. Marilyn from Orange County said that her supervisor openly watched porn on his computer. Others reported that their supervisors had taken pictures of their chests or behinds on their phones and sent them to their male co-workers. None of the women knew that this could be considered sexual harassment. They said, "I didn't realize that's harassment because he didn't actually touch me," Valles, the union leader, says. They thought that this was "just the culture of buildings at night."

Even the definition of rape was not clear to some of the women. Many were not aware that rape includes many forms of physical abuse with penetration—and the group had a difficult but illuminating discussion about the legal definition of the crime. "What I learned from some of the deep, quality training we did was that there was a real lack of education and that once you know what sexual harassment is, that it does make a difference," says Valles, who participated in the first *promotora* training.

García of the Maintenance Cooperation Trust Fund was part of the first training as well, and she says that once the group was given answers and information, they were visibly elevated and empowered. By helping the women realize that sexual harassment and assault were neither acceptable nor legal, the training helped them cast out feelings of shame, García says. "It's like when you've been told a lie your whole life and it's that moment when you realize it's a lie, and you are not bound by that untruth," she says. "So all of the limitations that you felt when you were taught that lie, you become unshackled and released from them."

The first group of *promotoras* had not yet finished their training when they were presented with an opportunity to put it into action. After Georgina Hernández had made her call to action on sexual violence at the wage-theft law celebration, the policy arm of the union had begun seeking ways to address the problem. These leaders approached Lorena González-Fletcher, a Democratic state legislator from San Diego who had previously been a union organizer. González-Fletcher agreed to work with the janitors' union, the SEIU California State Council, and Equal Rights Advocates, the organization that had represented María Bojórquez in her lawsuit against ABM, to draft and introduce a bill specifically to rein in abuses in the janitorial industry.[15]

Neither the union nor the Maintenance Cooperation Trust Fund had planned it this way, but through the *promotora* program, there was a group of activated female janitors who were ready to hold themselves up as examples of why the bill was necessary. "It was very organic," says García. "I wish I could tell you we had a grandiose plan. But frankly, this was uncharted territory for both organizations."

As the bill was discussed and debated in hearings and caucus meetings, janitor after janitor came forward to testify about sexual attacks on the night shift. Some were sharing their stories for the first time publicly. Some, like Leticia Soto, had only just begun to admit aloud that they were rape survivors. Soto had come to the United States in 2004 and she took a job as a janitor to support her three children. After three years in the country, she found herself working for a predatory supervisor. For nearly a decade, she had never said a word about being punched, bitten, and scratched by her supervisor as he raped her, repeatedly, after she had clocked in for work.

Soto was a member of the first *promotora* group with Georgina Hernández, and that training, coupled with the invitation to speak with legislators, pushed her to finally tell her teenage daughter she had been sexually harassed. Days later, at an event with legislators, Soto offered public testimony in support of the bill and shared her personal account of rape at work.

While the bill worked its way through the legislative process, the *promotoras* took their activism outside the halls of the statehouse with the goal of bringing visibility to workplace sexual assault. In Sacramento, they blocked traffic at an intersection near the capitol, unfurling a banner that said, END RAPE ON THE NIGHT SHIFT. The union organized rallies and marches in the San Francisco Bay Area, Los Angeles, and San Diego, where workers held up signs that said STOP THE RAPE and YA BASTA. They held screenings of the "Rape on the Night Shift" documentary throughout the state, and *promotoras* attended to hold up personalized signs like I KEPT SILENT BECAUSE I DIDN'T WANT MY KIDS TO KNOW or I STAYED SILENT BECAUSE NOBODY CAN HEAR YOU WHEN YOU WORK ALONE AT NIGHT. At speak-outs during these public events, women took turns telling their stories of harassment and abuse on the job.

In the final week before the end of the California legislative session, the union and the *promotoras* were still out in the streets making noise. The bill's final version required janitorial companies to register with the state so that government inspectors could track the labor conditions at the smallest and hardest-to-reach companies like the one Georgina Hernández had worked for. It also called on janitorial companies to provide sexual harassment training to all workers.

After passing both houses of the state legislature, the bill now sat on Governor Jerry Brown's desk, awaiting an unclear fate. Under California law, the governor has thirty days to sign a bill and give it his official endorsement. If he did nothing, the bill would still automatically become law.

What the *promotoras* worried about was a veto. The opposition to the bill by influential business organizations had softened, but like the domestic workers demanding worker protections in statehouses throughout the country, the *promotoras* worried that because they were disenfranchised workers and voters, the governor was not going to prioritize their cause.

To keep the pressure on, the union and the *promotoras* decided to stage a hunger strike in front of the state capitol on the five days leading up to the governor's deadline to sign the bill.

On a Monday morning in September, more than a half-dozen female janitors assembled on a shady patch of grass near the capitol to begin the fast. In the mornings, that day and each day for the rest of the week, the women met with supporters. In the afternoons, as their energy began to wane, they rested before holding a spiritual ceremony to close out each day. Each evening, they slept at a local church, returning to the capitol lawn in the morning to resume their vigil.

Georgina Hernández had come to the hunger strike with her young daughter, who played among the chairs and blankets arranged on the grass. She couldn't fast because she was pregnant but she sat with the others in solidarity. As in the fight for wage-theft legislation, Hernández had been a frequent presence in Sacramento and at events throughout the state to support the bill to combat workplace sexual assault. Just weeks before, at a community event in Oakland to rally support for the legislation, she'd stood at the front of the room holding up a sign that said, I KEPT SILENT SO I COULD FEED MY KIDS, and another that said, I KEPT SILENT BECAUSE I WAS ASHAMED.

For years those pressures had kept Hernández mute, but the Maintenance Cooperation Trust Fund had shown her that she could demand redress. Her *promotora* training, which had yielded a community of confidantes, had helped Hernández translate her trauma into action. "Now when I see a woman in the street in tears, I walk up to her and ask her if she's okay," Hernández says. "If she is experiencing violence, I tell her it doesn't have to be like that—join us."

On the afternoon of their fourth day of fasting, the sun had begun to drop behind the horizon when the group saw a woman in a business suit walking purposefully toward them with a cell phone in her hand. When she reached the *promotoras'* encampment, the woman told them that she worked for the governor's office, and just moments ago, the governor had signed into law the bill dedicated to curbing sexual harassment and assault on the night shift. On her phone, she showed them a picture of the document with the governor's signature at the bottom, and everyone crowded around to look.

There was a single beat of stunned silence before the women collapsed into a teary group hug. In a cry that emerged as if from instinct, the women began to spontaneously chant, "*¡Sí se pudo! ¡Sí se pudo!*" Yes we did! Yes we did!

Valles says this effort to curb sexual harassment and violence has shown her that unions need to address the working conditions of its members more holistically and that organized labor can step outside of traditional advocacy strategies. More important, she says, it was a reminder that unions should remain ever vigilant by listening to their members: "This issue had existed and it wasn't until women in the union, through their own experiences and through collective action, that they felt more empowered to lead on this issue."

These efforts have inspired other locals of the Service Employees International Union to start similar legislative efforts for sexual harassment prevention in Seattle and Portland. UNITE HERE, the union that represents hotel workers, has also become proactive in pushing for local laws that would protect hotel cleaners and casino workers from sexual harassment and assault. In the fall of 2016, for example, workers in Seattle helped pass a local ordinance that gave housekeepers panic buttons for use in case of emergency. Following activism by the local union, the city of Chicago followed suit a year later.

A coalition of unions, worker organizations, and anti-violence groups have since come together to seek broader strategies for addressing harassment and assault at work. The coalition emerged out of the janitorial workers' efforts and calls itself the Ya Basta Coalition, the Enough Is Enough Coalition.[16] Its focus, however, is inclusive and comprehensive. "This is bigger than janitors," says García of the Maintenance Cooperation Trust Fund, which is a member of the coalition. "I know that restaurant advocates have taken this on, the garment industry, there are stories about sexual assault in domestic work. Society blames the victims and we are looking to expose and eliminate that."

After the word came down that the governor had signed the bill, Hernández and the other *promotoras* reveled in their victory on the capitol lawn as the sun went down. When the euphoria had worn off, some of the women suggested they continue their hunger strike until the next day at noon, as they had originally planned. There was some rousing commentary about how the hunger strike wasn't just about the legislation—it was also about reclaiming control over their bodies. The idea caught on with five of the women, who went back to the church with empty stomachs for one more night's rest.

The next day, the entire group assembled for the last time on the capitol lawn. Noon arrived quickly for Hernández. With the sun high in the sky, the group held a ceremony to close the event. All of the women had written letters to their attackers on the van ride from Southern California to Sacramento, and one by one they read them aloud before ripping them up and placing them into a circle of stones they had created on the capitol lawn. Farmworker organizer

Dolores Huerta offered a closing prayer. Then, each woman released a white dove, an idea that had come from Hernández.

Alejandra Valles, the janitor union's secretary-treasurer, said that in her work battling and excavating one of the most taboo topics among immigrant workers, she learned a crucial lesson about why women like Hernández are especially hesitant to talk about sexual violence at work. To start, there is the predictable list of barriers: fear of losing their jobs, fear of being blamed by their husbands or partners, and the immutable sense of shame. They're terrified of what it might feel like to talk about the assault, and they have real concerns about what it would mean for their safety. They worry about what would happen to their families if they are deported as a result of coming forward.

Then, for women like Hernández, who were desperate and driven enough to cross borders to leave impoverished and violent homes, there is one more complication to add to the list: "You have to ask how they were living before they got here," Valles says.

The union leader says that she has heard from women who, before being sexually assaulted at work, had been held captive by gangs in their home country, abused by their husbands, or raped when crossing the border. Then, once they find jobs in the United States and their supervisors or co-workers assault them, Valles says, they're told, "'Just shut up and be quiet—you already have it better than you had it before.' You get used to your own body being raped and you become numb to that. And those who are willing to exploit women in this situation know it."

The work that needs to be done now, she says, is to convey to these women that even if it is seemingly better than before, none of the abuse is acceptable. And the abusers need to understand that there are consequences for their actions and that "it's not okay to exploit someone because they've had it worse," she says.

Georgina Hernández had already survived so much by the time she arrived at a job to clean the hotel lobby near the Los Angeles airport. Her life had been branded by poverty, physical abuse, and self-sacrifice. Trauma had been layered upon itself until it had been pressed into the core of her. Still, she had found a way to refuse defeat. With every rally she attended, every meeting with the *promotoras*, every decision she made to share her story, she had gotten a little bit of relief. It was like letting out a little bit of internal pressure, like finally exhaling.

Hernández hadn't had a chance to learn to read or write, so when she had been asked to write a letter to her attacker, she had asked the union's Sandra Díaz and another *promotora* to help her put down her thoughts as she dictated.

"I survived," Hernández had begun. "I used to believe I was the only one / But we are thousands and thousands of women who have endured this fear / It was not easy to break our silence / The first time I couldn't even get the words out but I'm not afraid anymore, I'm not ashamed anymore."

Hernández had found these words on the long road from inexorable silence to the recognition that she was more than the worst things that had happened to her. It wasn't a coincidence that she had been the one who had requested that each woman release a dove to close the hunger strike—the realization that she could banish the shame she had harbored for so long had given her the sensation that comes with releasing a bird to the sky.

"Today," she had said aloud for one of the first times in her life, "I know it was not my fault."

Epilogue

The full text of Georgina Hernández's letter to her attacker:

I survived

I used to believe I was the only one
But we are thousands and thousands of women who have endured
    this fear
It was not easy to break our silence
The first time I couldn't even get the words out but I'm not afraid
    anymore, I'm not ashamed anymore
Today I know it was not my fault

I survived
Since girlhood I've borne this pain, I thought the world was cruel
You made me lose my dreams
My life became a nightmare, where I distrusted even my shadow
With such disgust I recall the first, second, and third time you
    took me as if I were a dessert
You humiliated me as if I were an animal
You were like a lion, awaiting your prey

I survived
Today I know we are many

Today I know that when I broke my silence I joined many who
   had done the same
Today I know I am not alone
Today I know it was not my fault
And today I say with my head held high that I feel no shame
Today I ask God to bless you and forgive you so you never do this
   to anyone again

I survived
I am here as a *Promotora*
I am here as a woman who dreams of changing the world
I am here as a Rape Survivor
Today I tell you smiling that I have begun to heal and that I begin
   a new era, guided by love for my daughter and for the new hope
   that will come soon
I am here with all of you and with my heart brimming with pride
   I tell you, We did it

El texto completo de la carta de Georgina Hernández a su agresor:

Sobreviví

Antes yo pensaba que era la única
Pero somos miles y miles de mujeres que han pasado por este
   miedo
No fue fácil romper el silencio
La primera vez ni me salía el habla pero ahora ya no tengo miedo,
   ya no tengo vergüenza
Hoy sé que no fue mi culpa

Sobreviví
Desde niña vengo cargando este dolor, yo pensaba que el mundo
   era cruel

Tú me hiciste perder mis sueños
Mi vida se convirtió en una pesadilla, donde desconfiaba hasta de
   mi sombra
Con que asco me acuerdo de la primera, segunda y tercera vez
   que me tomaste como si yo fuera un postre
Me humillaste como si fuera un animal
Eras como un león, esperando a tu presa

Sobreviví
Hoy sé que somos muchas
Hoy sé que cuando rompí el silencio me uní a muchas que tan
   bien lo hacían
Hoy sé que no estoy sola
Hoy sé que no fue mi culpa
Y hoy digo con la frente bien en alto que no siento vergüenza
Hoy pido a dios que te bendiga y que te perdone para que nunca
   más vuelvas a hacerle esto a nadie

Sobreviví
Estoy aquí como Promotora
Estoy aquí como una mujer que sueña con cambiar el mundo
Estoy aquí como una Sobreviviente de Violación
Hoy les digo sonriendo que he empezado a sanar y que empiezo
   una nueva etapa, donde me guía el amor a mi hija y a la nueva
   esperanza que vendrá pronto
Estoy aquí con todas ustedes y con el corazón lleno de orgullo les
   digo, Lo hicimos

Acknowledgments

This book is a testament to the power of collaboration. It emerged from years of teamwork, from the seemingly improbable scenario where journalists from various news organizations came together to produce long-form pieces for print, radio, and television, in both English and Spanish, on a topic that no one seemed to want to acknowledge or talk about.

The projects that resulted from this work, "Rape in the Fields" (2013) and "Rape on the Night Shift" (2015), were possible because organizations like UC Berkeley's Investigative Reporting Program, KQED-FM, PBS *Frontline*, Univision, and The Center for Investigative Reporting, where I work, came together to tackle challenging and resource-intensive reporting.

These projects serve as the foundation of this book, and my heartfelt thanks go to Linsay Rousseau Burnett, who originated this line of reporting, and to both Lowell Bergman and Andrés Cediel, who were crucial in initiating these collaborative investigations.

I am also forever indebted to the core reporting team from both projects: Daffodil Altan, Lowell Bergman, Andrés Cediel, Sasha Khokha, Hannah Mintz, Lauren Rosenfeld, Grace Rubenstein, and Nadine Sebai. It was a pleasure to work with professionals and humans of such exceptional caliber. I feel fortunate that in the process of poring over court records in our cubicles, shadowing night-shift janitors in Southern California, and embedding ourselves in the apple orchards of Eastern Washington, I have also found life-long friends.

I am also grateful for the editorial guidance we received in helping shape, refine, and vet the initial reporting on which a good portion of this book is based, especially from Judy Alexander, Raney Aronson-Rath, Ingrid Becker, Gary Bostwick, Andrew Donohue, Mark Katches, Isaac Lee, Tim McGirk, Richard C. Paddock, Susanne Reber and Bob Salladay.

It has been deeply rewarding to expand upon this reporting by writing this book, and I extend my sincerest thanks to zakia henderson-brown, my editor at The New Press, for giving me this opportunity—and for offering such thoughtful and patient guidance throughout the process.

This book would not be possible without the moral support of my friends and family. I am especially thankful for my partner, Javier, whose encouragement and home cooking kept me fortified when I felt adrift in a tsunami of words and unfinished thoughts.

Last but certainly not least, I hold the deepest appreciation for the women workers at the center of this reporting. As a journalist, I am keenly aware that I serve as an intermediary to those who have critical stories to tell. I cannot thank enough the many women who have been so generous and brave in helping illuminate and humanize a long-buried problem. I stand in awe of their power and resilience.

Notes

Introduction: The Weight of Silence

1. A compendium in English of our reporting for "Rape in the Fields" can be found at https://www.revealnews.org/article/female-workers-face-rape -harassment-in-us-agriculture-industry, at www.pbs.org/wgbh/frontline/film /rape-in-the-fields, and at ww2.kqed.org/forum/2013/06/25/rape-in-the-fields -an-investigation-into-the-sexual-assault-of-female-agricultural-workers.

2. Our reporting in English for "Rape on the Night Shift" can be found at www.revealnews.org/nightshift, at www.pbs.org/wgbh/frontline/film/rape -on-the-night-shift, and at https://ww2.kqed.org/news/tag/rape-on-the-night -shift.

3. Kimberlé Crenshaw, "Mapping the Margins: Intersectionality, Identity Politics, and Violence Against Women of Color," *Stanford Law Review* 43, no. 6 (July 1991): 1241–99.

4. Sexual harassment and violence at work happen in all industries and affect both sexes and all gender identities, as evidenced by press accounts and the docket of sexual harassment claims in federal and state courts. This book, however, focuses on sexual violence against immigrant women in low-wage jobs, a phenomenon that has been underreported.

1. Finding the Most Invisible Cases

1. See the State of California Department of Industrial Relations press release on this case, "California Labor Commissioner Cites Two Janitorial Companies More Than $1.5 Million for Multiple Wage Theft Violations," May 8, 2014, www.dir.ca.gov/DIRNews/2014/2014-42.pdf.

2. The supervisor was named in the lawsuit but was never served. The settlement resolved the entire case.

3. Helen Chen, Alejandra Domenzain, and Karen Andrews, "The Perfect Storm: How Supervisors Get Away with Sexually Harassing Workers Who

Work Alone at Night," Labor Occupational Health Program, UC Berkeley, May 2016, http://lohp.org/the-perfect-storm.

4. Sara Hinkley, Annette Bernhardt and Sarah Thomason, "Race to the Bottom: How Low-Road Subcontracting Affects Working Conditions in California's Property Services Industry," Labor Center, UC Berkeley, Mar. 8, 2016, http://laborcenter.berkeley.edu/race-to-the-bottom.

5. The mean wage for janitors cleaning buildings and dwellings in 2016, Bureau of Labor Statistics, www.bls.gov/oes/current/oes372011.htm.

6. Additional background and information about the campaign is available via the UCLA Labor Center's "Justice for Janitors" webpage, www.labor.ucla.edu/what-we-do/labor-studies/research-tools/campaigns-and-research/justice-for-janitors.

7. Based on a custom data run by the Department of Justice's Bureau of Justice Statistics. See also Erika Harrell, "Special Report: Workplace Violence 1992–2009," Bureau of Justice Statistics, Mar. 2011, www.bjs.gov/content/pub/pdf/wv09.pdf.

8. On July 5, 2016, the U.S. Labor Department's Occupational Safety and Health Administration fined Epic Health Services $98,000: www.osha.gov/news/newsreleases/region3/07052016.

9. In 2016, the U.S. Equal Employment Opportunity Commission received 6,758 complaints (or "charges") of sexual harassment. That year, the commission filed 46 lawsuits related to alleged violations of Title VII of The Civil Rights Act of 1964, which prohibits employment discrimination on the basis of race, color, religion, sex, and national origin.

2. The Open Secret

1. The accounts of assault and harassment at Evans Fruit are based on law enforcement records, as well as documents and testimony obtained through the litigation of *Equal Employment Opportunity Commission v. Evans Fruit Co Inc.*, filed in U.S. District Court in the Eastern District of Washington, civil case no. 2:10-cv-03033. The case was appealed to the U.S. Court of Appeals for the Ninth Circuit, case nos. 13-35886 and 13-35885, and settled in January 2016.

2. Mary Bauer and Mónica Ramírez, "Injustice on Our Plates: Immigrant Women in the U.S. Food Industry," Southern Poverty Law Center, Nov. 7, 2010, www.splcenter.org/20101108/injustice-our-plates.

3. Grace Meng et al., "Cultivating Fear: The Vulnerability of Immigrant Farmworkers in the US to Sexual Violence and Sexual Harassment," Human Rights Watch, May 15, 2012, www.hrw.org/news/2012/05/15/us-sexual-violence-harassment-immigrant-farmworkers.

4. Irma Morales Waugh, "Examining the Sexual Harassment Experiences of Mexican Immigrant Farmworking Women," *Violence Against Women* 16, no. 3 (Mar. 2010): 237–61.

5. ASISTA provided the surveys to The Center for Investigative Reporting, and Grace Rubenstein analyzed the results, which we published in an infographic accompanying our article: Bernice Yeung and Grace Rubenstein, "Female Workers Face Rape, Harassment in US Agriculture Industry," https://www.revealnews.org/article/female-workers-face-rape-harassment-in -us-agriculture-industry.

6. See *EEOC v. Tanimura & Antle*, 5:99-cv-20088-JW (N.D. Cal.).

7. In our reporting on sexual harassment litigation as it related to farm workers and janitors, we spoke with numerous attorneys who represented employers in various industries. They said that the cost of litigation often prompted employers to settle even those cases that the companies believed they could win in court, and that most settlement agreements clearly state that the employer doesn't admit wrongdoing.

8. See *EEOC v Austin J. DeCoster (d/b/a DeCoster Farms of IA) and Iowa Ag LLC*, 3:02-cv-03077-MWB (N.D. Iowa).

9. See *EEOC v. Moreno Farms, Inc.*, 1:2014-cv-23181 ((S.D. Fla.)

10. See *EEOC v. Harris Farms, Inc.*, F-02-6199-AWI LJO (E.D. Cal.)

11. The appeal, No. 05-16945, was heard by the Ninth Circuit Court of Appeals.

12. Tim Evans reportedly investigated the claims but he died of cancer in 2010. Since he did not document it, little is known about it.

13. Bill Evans passed away in December 2016 at age 87.

3. Behind Closed Doors and Without a Safety Net

1. Immigration Reform and Control Act of 1986, Pub. L. 99-603, 100 Stat. 3445.

2. Juan F. Perea, "The Echoes of Slavery: Recognizing the Racist Origins of the Agricultural and Domestic Worker Exclusion from the National Labor Relations Act," *Ohio State Law Journal* 72, no. 1 (Jan. 2011): 95–138.

3. Hina B. Shah and Marci Seville, "Domestic Worker Organizing: Building a Contemporary Movement for Dignity and Power," *Albany Law Review* 75, no. 1 (Jan. 2012): 413–46.

4. Premilla Nadasen, *Household Workers Unite: The Untold Story of African American Women Who Built a Movement* (Boston: Beacon Press, 2015); Premilla Nadasen, "Citizenship Rights, Domestic Work, and the Fair Labor Standards Act," *Journal of Policy History* 24, no. 1 (Jan. 2012): 74–94.

5. The U.S. Equal Employment Opportunity Commission has interpreted its obligations under Title VII of the Civil Rights Act of 1964 to include protecting workers from discrimination based on gender identity and sexual orientation. However, this is not a settled issue. *Masterpiece Cakeshop v. Colorado Civil Rights Commission* No. 16-111 was accepted by the U.S. Supreme Court for review, and the outcome will help decide whether laws

around religious freedom trump antidiscrimination laws related to sexual orientation. In addition, the U.S. Department of Justice has filed an amicus brief in *Zarda v. Altitude Express* that essentially argues that under federal law, it is not illegal to fire an employee based on his or her sexual orientation. Finally, Attorney General Jeff Sessions issued a memo in October 2017 that states that Title VII of the 1964 Civil Rights Act does not protect transgender workers from discrimination, in contrast to guidance issued by the Obama administration.

6. Nadasen, "Citizenship Rights, Domestic Work, and the Fair Labor Standards Act."

7. Ibid.

8. Ibid.

9. In addition to surveys and reports published by the National Domestic Workers Alliance, I found the qualitative studies by academics Pierrette Hondagneu-Sotelo of the University of Southern California and Mary Romero of Arizona State University especially instructive and illuminating. Pierrette Hondagneu-Soto, *Doméstica* (Berkeley: University of California Press, 2001); and Mary Romero, *Maid in the U.S.A.* (New York: Routledge, 1992).

10. Sameera Hafiz and Michael Paarlberg, "The Human Trafficking of Domestic Workers in the United States: Findings from the Beyond Survival Campaign," Institute for Policy Studies and National Domestic Workers Alliance, 2017, www.domesticworkers.org/sites/default/files/bs_report2017.pdf; and U.S. Government Accountability Office, "U.S. Government's Efforts to Address Alleged Abuse of Household Workers by Foreign Diplomats with Immunity Could Be Strengthened," Report to Senate Judiciary Committee Subcommittee on Human Rights and Law, July 2008, www.gao.gov/new .items/d08892.pdf.

11. See *United States of America v. Ngozi Nnaji and Emmanuel Nnaji*, 4:09-CR-172-A (N. Dist. Tex). The couple was convicted and Ngozi Nnaji received a prison sentence of nine years and Emmanuel Nnaji received a sentence of twenty years. They were also ordered to pay restitution of nearly $306,000 to their abused domestic worker.

12. Remark made at trial by Hon. John McBryde in *USA v. Ngozi Nnaji and Emmanuel Nnaji*.

13. Hondagneu-Sotelo, *Domésticas*, 30–37; Romero, *Maid in the U.S.A.*, 1–6, 61–63; Linda Burnham and Nik Theodore, "Home Economics: The Invisible and Unregulated World of Domestic Work"; and Nik Theodore, Beth Gutelius, and Linda Burnham, "HomeTruths: Domestic Workers in California," www.datacenter.org/wp-content/uploads/HomeTruths.pdf.

14. Burnham and Theodore, "Home Economics."

15. In addition to the Domestic Workers United, the coalition was made up of Adhikaar for Human Rights, Unity Housecleaners, Damayan Migrant

Workers Association, Haitian Women for Haitian Refugees, and Andolan—Organizing South Asian Workers.

16. Patrick Healy, "At Rally for Domestics' Rights, a Nanny Tells of Mistreatment," *New York Times*, Mar. 8, 2004.

17. Mujeres Unidas y Activas, Day Labor Program Women's Collective of La Raza Centro Legal, and DataCenter, "Behind Closed Doors: Working Conditions of California Household Workers," Mar. 2007, www.datacenter.org/wp-content/uploads/behindcloseddoors.pdf.

18. The California Domestic Workers Coalition was made up of Alianza de Mujeres Activas y Solidarias (ALMAS), La Colectiva de Mujeres de San Francisco, Mujeres Unidas y Activas, Filipino Advocates for Justice, Pilipino Workers Center, Coalition for Humane Immigrant Rights of Los Angeles, Instituto de Educación Popular del Sur de California, California Immigrant Policy Center, and Hand in Hand: The Domestic Employer Network.

4. When Only the Police and the Prosecutor Believe You

1. The description of the circumstances surrounding Guadalupe Chávez's rape allegations are based on law enforcement records and trial transcripts from the criminal prosecution of her case. The accused supervisor was acquitted.

2. There is an extensive literature on self-blame by sexual assault victims. The National Institute of Justice specifically cites: Janice Du Mont, Karen-Lee Miller, and Terri L. Myhr, "The Role of 'Real Rape' and 'Real Victim' Stereotypes in the Police Reporting Practices of Sexually Assaulted Women," *Violence Against Women* 9, no. 4 (Apr. 2003): 466–86.

3. Ibid.

4. U.S. Department of Justice Civil Rights Division, "Investigation of the Baltimore City Police Department," Aug. 10, 2016.

5. Robert C. Davis, Edna Erez, and Nancy Avitabile, "Access to Justice for Immigrants Who Are Victimized: The Perspectives of Police and Prosecutors," *Criminal Justice Policy Review* 12, no. 3 (Jan. 2001): 183–96.

6. Robert C. Davis and Nicole J. Hendricks, "Immigrants and Law Enforcement: A Comparison of Native-Born and Foreign-Born Americans' Opinions of the Police," *International Review of Victimology* 14, no. 1 (Jan. 2007): 81–94.

7. Jill Messing et al., "Latinas' Perceptions of Law Enforcement: Fear of Deportation, Crime Reporting, and Trust in the System," *Affilia* 30, no. 3 (Mar. 2015): 328–340.

8. See Carlos A. Cuevas and Chiara Sabina, "Final Report: Sexual Assault Among Latinas (SALAS) Study," National Criminal Justice Reference Service, Apr. 2010, www.ncjrs.gov/pdffiles1/nij/grants/230445.pdf.

9. Ibid.

10. Bernice Yeung, "Under Cover of Darkness, Female Janitors Face Rape and Assault," The Center for Investigative Reporting, June 23, 2015. See also Bernice Yeung and Grace Rubenstein, "Female Workers Face Rape, Harassment in US Agriculture Industry," The Center for Investigative Reporting, June 25, 2013.

11. This case is documented in greater detail in Yeung, "Under Cover of Darkness," and the court file related to this federal case, U.S. Equal Employment Opportunity Commission v. ABM Industries, which was settled in 2010.

12. Estelle B. Freedman, Redefining Rape: Sexual Violence in the Era of Suffrage and Segregation (Cambridge, MA: Harvard University Press, 2013).

13. Ibid.

14. A discussion of the various state laws and case law that required corroboration for rape is discussed here: Irving Younger, "The Requirement of Corroboration in Prosecutions for Sex Offenses in New York," Fordham Law Review 40, no. 2 (1971), 263–67.

15. According to Black's Law Dictionary, chastity is defined as "Purity; continence. That virtue which prevents the unlawful intercourse of the sexes. Also the slate of purity or abstinence from unlawful sexual connection." People v. Brown, 71 Hun 601, 24 N.Y. Supp. 1111; People v. Kehoe, 123 Cal. 224, 55 Pac. 911, 69 Am. St. Rep. 52; and State v. Carron, 18 Iowa 375, 87 Am. Dec. 401.

16. Patricia J. Falk, "'Because Ladies Lie': Eliminating Vestiges of the Corroboration and Resistance Requirements from Ohio's Sexual Offenses," Cleveland State Law Review 62 (2014): 343.

17. National District Attorneys Association, "Rape Shield Statutes as of March 2011," www.ndaa.org/pdf/NCPCA%20Rape%20Shield%202011.pdf.

18. Susannah Meadows, "What Really Happened That Night at Duke," Newsweek, Apr. 22, 2007.

19. Kimberly A. Lonsway, Joanne Archambault, and David Lisak, "False Reports: Moving Beyond the Issue to Successfully Investigate and Prosecute Non-stranger Sexual Assault," The Voice 3, no. 1 (Jan. 2009), 1–11; David Lisak et al., "False Allegations of Sexual Assault: An Analysis of Ten Years of Reported Cases," Violence Against Women 16, no. 12 (Dec. 2010), 1318–34; Melanie Heenan and Suellen Murray, "Study of Reported Rapes in Victoria 2000–2003: Summary Research Report," Statewide Steering Committee to Reduce Sexual Assault, 2006; and Kimberly Lonsway, "Trying to Move the Elephant in the Room: Responding to the Challenge of False Rape Reports," Violence Against Women 16, no. 12 (Dec. 2010), 1356–71.

20. Lisak et. al., "False Allegations of Sexual Assault."

21. This issue is highlighted through a systematic review of unfounded cases in Baltimore following a newspaper report that identified problems with

the way that rapes were being classified by police. Baltimore City Sexual Assault Response Team, "October 5, 2011, Annual Report," mcasa.org/_mcasa
Web/wp-content/uploads/2011/11/BaltimoreCityAnnualReport_print.pdf.
There have been a number of additional news reports on the misclassification
of rape cases, e.g., Alex Campbell, "Unfounded," *Buzzfeed*, Sept. 8, 2016; and
another in-depth example: Robyn Doolittle, "Unfounded: Why Police Dismiss 1 in 5 Sexual Assault Claims as Baseless," *The Globe and Mail*, Feb. 3,
2017.

22. Lonsway, Archambault, and Lisak, "False Reports."

23. Ibid.

24. Ibid.

25. Ibid.

26. Ibid.

27. National estimate based on crime and criminal justice data analyzed by
the Rape, Abuse & Incest National Network (RAINN). These statistics can
be viewed here: https://www.rainn.org/statistics/criminal-justice-system. The
methodology behind these statistics is explained here: https://www.rainn
.org/about-rainns-statistics. Professors Cassia Spohn of Arizona State University and Linda M. Williams of Wellesley College and University of Massachusetts–Lowell have also done detailed studies on the attrition of sexual
assault cases in specific jurisdictions.

28. Jen Fifield, "Despite Concerns, Sex Offenders Face New Restrictions,"
Stateline, Pew Charitable Trusts, May 6, 2016.

29. Ibid. See also: Elizabeth Erhardt Mustaine, "Sex Offender Residency
Restrictions: Successful Integration or Exclusion?" *Criminology and Public
Policy* 13, no. 1 (Jan. 2014): 169–77.

30. Analysis of data on exonerations by year and type of crime obtained
from the National Registry of Exonerations, a project of University of
California–Irvine and the University of Michigan, www.law.umich.edu/spe
cial/exoneration/Pages/Exoneration-by-Year-Crime-Type.aspx.

31. Siddhartha Bandyopadhyay and Bryan C. McCannon, "The Effect of
the Election of Prosecutors on Criminal Trials," University of Birmingham
Department of Economics Discussion Paper 11-08, Mar. 10, 2011, pp. 1–2.

32. Ibid.

33. AEquitas, the Justice Management Institute, and the Urban Institute, "Model Response to Sexual Violence for Prosecutors: An Invitation to
Lead," 2017, www.aequitasresource.org/Model-Response-to-Sexual-Violence
-for-Prosecutors-RSVP-An-Invitation-to-Lead.pdf.

34. Ibid.

35. Ibid.

36. These accounts of rape are based on documents from the civil lawsuit,
Leticia Zúñiga Escamilla v. SMS Holdings Corporation; Service Management

Systems, Inc.; and Marco González, filed in U.S. District Court, District of Minnesota.

37. Rape, Abuse & Incest National Network, www.rainn.org/statistics /criminal-justice-system, and www.rainn.org/about-rainns-statistics.

5. All That We Already Know

1. U.S. Senate Committee on the Judiciary, "Hearings on the Nomination of Judge Clarence Thomas to Be Associate Judge of the Supreme Court of the United States," Oct. 11, 1991, part 4, J-102-40 (Washington: Government Printing Office, 1993), www.loc.gov/law/find/nominations/thomas/hearing -pt4.pdf.

2. Ibid.

3. Margo Jefferson, "The Thomas-Hill Question, Answered Anew," review of *Strange Justice: The Selling of Clarence Thomas*, by Jane Mayer and Jill Abramson, *New York Times*, Nov. 11, 1994.

4. This comment can be found in Part 4 of the transcript of the Hearings Before the Committee on the Judiciary, United States Senate, "Nomination of Judge Clarence Thomas To Be Associate Justice of the Supreme Court of the United States," October 11–13, 1991. Viewable at the Library of Congress: www.loc.gov/law/find/nominations/thomas/hearing-pt4.pdf.

5. This was an especially controversial moment in the already highly charged proceedings. It received wide media coverage, e.g., Andrew Rosenthal, "Psychiatry's Use in Thomas Battle Raises Ethics Issue," *New York Times*, October 20, 1991.

6. Amanda Cochran, "Anita Hill: Clarence Thomas Hearings 23 Years Ago Unfair," CBS News, Mar. 13, 2014; "Anita Hill: Biden Did 'Terrible Job' Running Clarence Thomas Hearings," *Talking Points Memo*, Mar. 20, 2014.

7. Cochran, "Anita Hill."

8. Jill Smolowe, "Sex, Lies and Politics: He Said, She Said," *Time*, Oct. 21, 1991.

9. Elizabeth Kolbert, "The Thomas Nomination: Most in National Survey Say Judge Is the More Believable," *New York Times*, Oct. 15, 1991.

10. Dennis Cauchon, "*USA Today* Poll: Whom Do You Believe? Testimony Shifts Support to Nominee," *USA Today*, Oct. 14, 1991.

11. Louise F. Fitzgerald et al., "The Incidence and Dimensions of Sexual Harassment in Academia and the Workplace," *Journal of Vocational Behavior* 32, no. 2 (Apr. 1988): 152–75.

12. The activities identified in the SEQ are based on the behavior of real people, though the names Fitzgerald uses here are not their actual names.

13. Barbara A. Gutek, Ryan O. Murphy, and Bambi Douma, "A Review and Critique of the Sexual Experiences Questionnaire (SEQ)," *Law and Human Behavior* 28, no. 4 (Aug. 2004): 457–82.

14. See Douglas D. Baker, David E. Terpstra, and Kinley Larntz, "The Influence of Individual Characteristics and Severity of Harassing Behavior on Reactions to Sexual Harassment," *Sex Roles* 22, no. 5–6 (Mar. 1990): 305–325; and David E. Terpstra and Douglas D. Baker, "The Identification and Classification of Reactions to Sexual Harassment," *Journal of Organizational Behavior* 10, no. 1 (Jan. 1989): 1–14.

15. Julie A. Woodzicka and Marianne LaFrance, "Real Versus Imagined Gender Harassment," *Journal of Social Issues* 57, no. 1 (Spring 2001): 15–30.

16. Louise F. Fitzgerald, Karla Fischer, and Suzanne Swan, "Why Didn't She Just Report Him? The Psychological and Legal Implications of Women's Responses to Sexual Harassment," *Journal of Social Issues* 51, no. 1 (Spring 1995): 117–38.

17. Another EEOC regional attorney, William R. Tamayo, also said that over the years he has consistently seen sexual harassment cases that involve allegations of retaliation.

18. Fitzgerald, Fischer, and Swan, "Why Didn't She Just Report Him?"

19. In farmwork: Jeanne Murphy et al., "'They Talk like That, but We Keep Working': Sexual Harassment and Sexual Assault Experiences Among Mexican Indigenous Farmworker Women in Oregon," *Journal of Immigrant and Minority Health* 17, no. 6 (Dec. 2015): 1834–39; in the military: Michelle A. Mengeling et al., "Reporting Sexual Assault in the Military: Who Reports and Why Most Servicewomen Don't," *American Journal of Preventive Medicine* 47, no. 1 (July 2014): 17–25; and in academia: Laurie A. Rudman, Eugene Borgida, and Barbara A. Robertson, "Suffering in Silence: Procedural Justice Versus Gender Socialization Issues in University Sexual Harassment Grievance Procedures," *Basic and Applied Social Psychology* 17 (1995), no. 4: 519–41.

20. Mindy E. Bergman et al., "The (Un)reasonableness of Reporting: Antecedents and Consequences of Reporting Sexual Harassment," *Journal of Applied Psychology* 87, no. 2 (May 2002): 230–42.

21. Kimberly A. Lonsway, Rebecca Paynich, and Jennifer N. Hall, "Sexual Harassment in Law Enforcement: Incidence, Impact, and Perception," *Police Quarterly* 16, no. 2 (June 2013): 177–210.

22. Beth E. Schneider, "Put Up and Shut Up: Workplace Sexual Assaults," *Gender and Society* 5, no. 4 (Dec. 1991), 533–48.

23. Neil M. Malamuth, Scott Haber, and Seymour Feshbach, "Testing Hypotheses Regarding Rape: Exposure to Sexual Violence, Sex Differences, and the 'Normality' of Rapists," *Journal of Research in Personality* 14, no. 1 (Mar. 1980): 121–37.

24. Neil M. Malamuth et al., "Characteristics of Aggressors Against Women: Testing a Model Using a National Sample of College Students," *Journal of Consulting and Clinical Psychology* 59, no. 5 (Nov. 1991): 670; and

Neil M. Malamuth, Christopher L. Heavey, and Daniel Linz, "Predicting Men's Antisocial Behavior Against Women: The Interaction Model of Sexual Aggression," in Gordon C. Nagayama Hall et al., ed., *Sexual Aggression: Issues in Etiology, Assessment and Treatment* (Washington, DC: Hemisphere, 1993), 63–97.

25. Neil M. Malamuth, "Rape Proclivity Among Males," *Journal of Social Issues* 37, no. 4 (Oct. 1981), 138–57.

26. Neil M. Malamuth et al., "Using the Confluence Model of Sexual Aggression to Predict Men's Conflict with Women: A 10-Year Follow-up Study," *Journal of Personality and Social Psychology* 69, no. 2 (Aug. 1995); 353.

27. John B. Pryor, "Sexual Harassment Proclivities in Men," *Sex Roles* 17, no. 5–6 (Sept. 1987): 269–90.

28. John B. Pryor, Christine M. LaVite, and Lynnette M. Stoller, "A Social Psychological Analysis of Sexual Harassment: The Person/Situation Interaction," *Journal of Vocational Behavior* 42, no. 1 (Feb. 1993): 68–83.

29. John B. Pryor, Janet L. Giedd, and Karen B. Williams, "A Social Psychological Model for Predicting Sexual Harassment," *Journal of Social Issues* 51, no. 1 (Spring 1995), 69–84.

30. John A. Bargh et al., "Attractiveness of the Underling: An Automatic Power? Sex Association and Its Consequences for Sexual Harassment and Aggression," *Journal of Personality and Social Psychology* 68, no. 5 (May 1995): 768–81.

31. Louise F. Fitzgerald et al., "Antecedents and Consequences of Sexual Harassment in Organizations: A Test of an Integrated Model," *Journal of Applied psychology* 82, no. 4 (Aug. 1997), 578–89; see also: Jill Hunter Williams, Louise F. Fitzgerald, and Fritz Drasgow, "The Effects of Organizational Practices on Sexual Harassment and Individual Outcomes in the Military," *Military Psychology* 11 (1999), no. 3: 303–28; and Charles L. Hulin, Louise F. Fitzgerald, and Fritz Drasgow, *Organizational Influences on Sexual Harassment* (Thousand Oaks, CA: Sage Publications, 1996).

32. Based on statistics from the U.S. Equal Employment Opportunity Commission, "Charges Alleging Sex-Based Harassment (Charges filed with EEOC) FY 2010–FY 2016," www.eeoc.gov/eeoc/statistics/enforcement/sexual_harassment_new.cfm. This data does not include sexual harassment reports made to state agencies.

6. The Ways Forward

1. The June 2016 report published by the EEOC summarizes the research on sexual harassment training: Chai R. Feldblum and Victoria A. Lipnic, *Report of the Select Task Force on the Study of Harassment in the Workplace*, www.eeoc.gov/eeoc/task_force/harassment/report.cfm. For studies more specifically of workplace training, see Shereen G. Bingham, and Lisa L. Scherer,

"The Unexpected Effects of a Sexual Harassment Educational Program," *Journal of Applied Behavioral Science* 37, no. 2 (June 2001): 125–53; and Vicki J. Magley et al., "Changing Sexual Harassment Within Organizations via Training Interventions: Suggestions and Empirical Data," in Ronald J. Burke & Cary L. Cooper, ed., *The Fulfilling Workplace: The Organization's Role in Achieving Individual and Organizational Health* (Surrey, UK: Gower, 2013), 225–46.

2. Feldblum and Lipnic, *Report of the Select Task Force on the Study of Harassment.*

3. Fair Foods Standards Council, "2015 Fair Food Program Annual Report," www.allianceforfairfood.org/news/2016/2/17/recently-released-and-available -for-download-the-2015-fair-food-program-annual-report.

4. Extreme physical sexual harassment is outlawed by Title VII of the Civil Rights Act of 1964, and as a result, some states and local jurisdictions require some employers to offer sexual harassment training that discusses rights and reporting. However, there are no federal standards that specifically spell out what employers must do to prevent on-the-job sexual assault or rape.

5. See: 12 New York Codes, Rules and Regulations, Part 800.6, Public Employer Workplace Violence Prevention Programs.

6. Washington State Department of Labor & Industries, Division of Occupational Safety and Health, "Workplace Violence: Awareness and Prevention for Employers and Employees," www.lni.wa.gov/IPUB/417-140-000.pdf.

7. These new policies emerged out of rule-making by California's Department of Industrial Relations, and the final text can be viewed here: www .dir.ca.gov/oshsb/documents/Workplace-Violence-Prevention-in-Health -Care-apprdtxt.pdf.

7. ¡Sí Se Pudo! Yes We Did!

1. Based on analysis of federal data from the U.S. Census: Survey of Small Business Owners, County Business Patterns, and Statistics of U.S. Businesses.

2. Nicole B. Porter, "Women, Unions, and Negotiation," *Nevada Law Journal* 14 (Spring 2014): 465–95.

3. Marion Crain and Ken Matheny, "Labor's Identity Crisis," *California Law Review* 89, no. 6 (Dec. 2001): 1767–1846.

4. Ibid.

5. Marion Crain and Ken Matheny, "Labor's Divided Ranks: Privilege and the United Front Ideology," *Cornell Law Review* 84, no. 6 (Sept. 1999): 1542–1626.

6. Marion Crain, "Between Feminism and Unionism: Working Class Women, Sex Equality, and Labor Speech," *Georgetown Law Journal* 82 (July 1994): 1903.

7. This statement was provided in 2015 as part of the Rape on the Night Shift reporting. Subsequent correspondence from the company to the author, sent in June 2015, reiterated that the company has state-of-the-art policies on investigating and handling sexual harassment complaints by its employees.

8. Though Georgina Hernández's sexual harassment lawsuit was filed against both the company she worked for and her supervisor, the case was resolved before the supervisor could be served. The settlement resolved the case for all parties.

9. Kim Bobo, *Wage Theft in America: Why Millions of Working Americans Are Not Getting Paid and What We Can Do About It* (New York: The New Press, 2011).

10. Human Impact Partners, UCLA Labor Center, and Restaurant Opportunities Center–Los Angeles, "Health Impact Assessment of the Proposed Los Angeles Wage Theft Ordinance," Aug. 2014, www.labor.ucla.edu/wp-content /uploads/downloads/2014/08/wage_theft_report_082514_KF.pdf.

11. Ibid.

12. California Senate Bill 588, "Employment: Nonpayment of wages: Labor Commissioner: Judgment Enforcement," 2015.

13. Brian Watt, "With Minimum Wage on the Rise, Labor Leaders Focus on Wage Theft," Southern California Public Radio, KPCC, Sept. 7, 2015.

14. Sara Hinkley, Annette Bernhardt, and Sarah Thomason, "Race to the Bottom: How Low-Road Subcontracting Affects Working Conditions in California's Property Services Industry," Labor Center, UC Berkeley, Mar. 8, 2016, laborcenter.berkeley.edu/race-to-the-bottom.

15. California Assembly Bill 1978, "Property Workers Protection Act," 2016.

16. The Ya Basta Coalition includes organizations such as Worksafe, Futures Without Violence, Equal Rights Advocates, the California Coalition Against Sexual Assault, the Maintenance Cooperation Trust Fund, SEIU United Workers West, and the University of California–Berkeley's Labor Occupational Health Program.

Index

About the Author

Bernice Yeung is an award-winning journalist for Reveal from The Center for Investigative Reporting. She was a 2015–2016 Knight-Wallace Fellow at the University of Michigan. Her work has appeared in the *New York Times*, *Mother Jones*, and *The Guardian*, as well as on KQED Public Radio and PBS *Frontline*. She lives in Berkeley, California.

Publishing in the Public Interest

Thank you for reading this book published by The New Press. The New Press is a nonprofit, public interest publisher. New Press books and authors play a crucial role in sparking conversations about the key political and social issues of our day.

We hope you enjoyed this book and that you will stay in touch with The New Press. Here are a few ways to stay up to date with our books, events, and the issues we cover:

- Sign up at www.thenewpress.com/subscribe to receive updates on New Press authors and issues and to be notified about local events
- Like us on Facebook: www.facebook.com/newpress books
- Follow us on Twitter: www.twitter.com/thenewpress

Please consider buying New Press books for yourself; for friends and family; or to donate to schools, libraries, community centers, prison libraries, and other organizations involved with the issues our authors write about.

The New Press is a 501(c)(3) nonprofit organization. You can also support our work with a tax-deductible gift by visiting www.thenewpress.com/donate.